By T.C. Cooksley

Secrets to Sell your Home

Secrets to Sell your House

Introduction

So, you want to sell your home for Top Dollar, FAST! A man with a plan is far better likely to succeed than a man with an idea and no goals, indeed!

I will not bore you with my life story in the pages of this How To Book. I will take a moment to assure you, I am a professional Realtor with years of experience. I began my real estate career in a 150 year old Savings and Loan. They have all been gone since 1989. And with their demise so too went my first retirement investment. We all learn as we go. I learned young that my future was my own. From there I worked in Underwriting for a number of years before moving into the Wholesale Lending Sale Executive area. For a few years I worked for a Mortgage Broker. They take applications, gather documentation and sell it to Wholesale Lenders. We had a crash in the early nineties in the New England States. What I learned from that experience… 'don't put all your eggs in one basket.' At that time I liked one lender, they were effected by the crash. Those underwriters who had spread their loans out did better than those that sent all their loans to one lender. When I became a Wholesale Sales Executive I was allowed more flexibility with my time and schedule.

Moving forward, my husband believed in the value of real estate and invested in a few rental properties, so I found myself in 'Property Management.' Then, a friend I had trained in mortgages at the Saving and Loan called an asked me to help her with a development she was working on. From there I went into Residential Real Estate in Fredericksburg, Virginia. As this was a lucrative market and unlike commercial you see a steady return for your efforts. I have remained predominantly in Residential Sales for the last fifteen years.

Are you skilled at selling homes for top dollar? Do you know how to set the price for your house?

If this is not something you do at least two or three times a year the answer to this question is generally, 'No.' Do you realize the average American does not know that your tax based value generally has nothing to do with the 'Market Value' of your home? 9 out of 10 homeowners do not even know how much they are paying in property tax annually or monthly! This is because the majority of homeowners have their taxes 'escrowed,' leaving the tax bill to their lender to pay along with their Homeowners Insurance premiums.

Lenders prefer it this way so they are not surprised by 'tax liens' or home loss due to fire not having a re-built coverage. In effect the lender wants to escrow your taxes and insurance to protect their interest. The only lien to supersede a Mortgage is a Tax Lien. Should your home catch fire without Homeowners Insurance in place the lender has no assurance their interest in the property can be re-cooped.

The job of selling a home can be daunting! Are you old enough to have admired the humor of Erma Bombeck? I wish I could say I'll make this book as witty and enjoyable as one of her books. But, I would be lying. What I will admit too is that as a Professional with years of experience this book offers you day to day common sense moments you may over look in your zeal of selling your property quickly and for top dollar. I have sprinkled throughout this books tidbits of experiences and knowledge I have developed along the way.

I am not a ghost writer filling a book with stats you can easily glean from the internet. It is my goal to show you a few pointers so that you understand that todays homebuyer is generally either looking for a clean, and tidy 'Ready to Move-In' home or they realized they can not afford the home of their dreams so they are looking for something they can fix up and make it their own. Those that are looking for minor repairs are looking for a deal, therefore, they will not pay top dollar. Those Ready to Move-in want a home that is spotless and well tended. They will pay top dollar to walk in a home that does not need any immediate repair. When pricing a home, you need to realistically look at your home and decide which category will you chose to be in.

I believe in the service of an experienced Realtor as opposed to a "Buy Me" Button online or Doing It Yourself. I have seen to many 'Flipped Homes' where doors and windows do not work properly to ever be impressed with the DYI mentality presently sweeping the Nation. That being said, I realize that ultimately how you sell your home is your decision. This book is to help you make wise decisions in where you spend or not spend your dollars to help you accomplish your goals.

Do you have the time, and energy to meet every perspective buyer? Do you enjoy having strangers rummage through your drawers and cabinets unsupervised? This book can help you understand the process and help you sell your home with perspective.

Sometimes every thing hinges on a Great First Impression! Selling a house is one of those things! You rarely get a second chance with a buyer. In today's competitive real estate marketplace we want perspective buyers to 'fall in love on-line!' How do Realtors help a Property Seller market that budding relationship that creates a forever relationship in those initial first seconds? It's really important that you work with your Realtor to create that first glimpse and make in memorable to a buyer.

Realize the sale doesn't just hinge on the interior of the house. There Must be 'Curb Appeal.' If you have the nicest home in the neighborhood, what can you do to mitigate the surrounding properties? Do you live on a badly maintained road? Do you realize how this will impact the value of your home?

Every Listing Agent knows you desire to find a home buyer who wants your home above all others! Making a striking home presentation that leaves a lasting impression in their minds above all the comparable presently for sale.

This is a book to help you sell your home successfully and quickly. An agent will touch on many of the same targets you find in this book. The more techniques and strategies you implement from this book the easier it will be to reach your desired price point and time schedule.

Many of these ideas have been used time and again by home Sellers to sell their home quickly and successfully. The more you follow these steps the smoother the transition will be. Discover the importance of understanding Market Value and realizing it has nothing to do with Tax Assessments. Why Zestimates may not come close to your homes price. What improvements have the best rate of return for your investment.

I truly hope this book will be of value and assistance to you. May this book help you make the most of your time and efforts to sell your house quickly at a good price. As a Real Estate Professional I am always happy to assist you with Market Analysis and a Marketing Plan custom to fit you and your lifestyle.

Pre-Listing Steps

Have you considered there are at least 170 Steps a Realtor goes through on each Listing they accept. It is not as simple a job as one may think. A Listing Realtor must be a Marketeer, as well as a Sales person and Excellent People Manager that is able to manage both the Seller, other agents and the public.

So, why should you use a Realtor to sell your home in today's Technology age? Why do you need a physical person available to help you? What do they offer that you will not get from a 'Make me Move Botton' on a website? It is crucial for a home seller to understand the factors that determine the price of a house. It's equally important to understand that real estate sales are still a 'Local Market' business. Using a Local Realtor that is familiar with your community will make a positive impact on the sale of your home. It will also avoid no showings because the listing agent isn't able to market to local agents. Or advise you to provide a full propane tank to the buyer without asking for re-payment for that propane at closing. It's an agent familiar with the homeowner association issues like water supplies and limited use of the vacant lot next door.

Familiarize yourself with real estate terms; do you know the difference between Market Value and Appraised Value vs Assessed Value? A great way to avoid disappointment and frustration is to understand 'home value' may be less than you expected your home to be worth. Avoid overpricing, that simply leaves you with an unsold property.

Once you accept your Castle may not sell for the ideal price you imagined you've reached step one! There is a difference between value to you, worth to the county in which you live and the price the market will bare.

Curious what your home is worth?

So, you're curious and want to do your own research before calling a Realtor. So you seek a Free Online Tool to provide you with a ball park estimate of your houses current value. Or you look on line to see what's For Sale in your neighborhood.

Why does this number not match up to that of a Realtor's Market Value or an Appraised Value? The online value relies on available data. There are many factors this algorithm does not take into account, such as; location, location and current market trends.

Additionally, What a home List for is no guarantee that is what it will Sell For. Consider homes that are listed by an Auctioneer in the MLS or online. They are generally listed for a fraction of their value. You expect that without question. You know if you attend the auction the home will sell for Far More than the advertised 'starting' bid price. A home for sale must have an "Asking Price". That is not always a realistic number. Some Seller's choose to chase the market. Others choose to be ahead of the market. It's up to you as an educated Seller to chose which one you are going to be.

The Professional Appraiser

A professional appraiser should be disinterested and licensed in the state your house is located in. These individual usually have at least an Associates Degree before committing to approximately 2000 hours of appraisal experience under the tutelage of an experienced Appraiser. They are suppose to be familiar with the area in which the house is located. I have interacted with many Appraisers over the years. Many are comfortable appraising within a 50 to 100 mile radius of their office. Beyond the 100 miles they are not comfortable appraising as the residential appraisal is based on more than just comparables. It's an Appraisers job to be certain they are good comparable. Sometimes you're on a country or school district line and one comp may not be truly comparable. An Appraisal relies greatly on the locate records, and appraisers general knowledge of any given area. Were there issues in the past that may effect the "Marketability" of one house on the street vs another, for example. There are other types of appraisals but for the purpose of this book I will only be considering residential appraising. A Residential Appraiser estimates the value of a house by examining the property inside and out. They consider the type of loan being used by the Buyer when purchasing the home. Some financing requires additional inspections by the appraiser. Some require additional documentation. The appraiser draws a floor plan while they walk through the property, and take photos of the interior and exterior. If there is a contract on your house when the appraisal is ordered they compare the sales price with similar homes in the area that have recently sold. An appraisal is 'subjective.' Three Appraisers may appraise the same property and come up with three different values, however, those values are generally within 10% of one another. An appraisal has a limited time value. (Meaning that what your home is worth in February may be different in MayTheir fees are generally between $400 - $750.

Assessed Value by The Tax Assessor

This number has nothing to do with the Market Value or the actual Appraised Value. It is based on the percentage of the appraised value for the purpose of the tax base. This is how the County budgets funds. 60% of American homeowners believe their homes are assessed too high. Please keep in mind, this does not reflect the homes sales price.

Market Analysis by a Realtor

Real Estate is a Relationship Business. This means that you should work with an agent that you feel comfortable with. I have never understood why people complain about their agent after they have paid them thousands of dollars. This is America! You are not forced to work with a particular agent you heard advertise on the radio. You chose to work with that agent or that team. This is an important, high dollar investment. Shouldn't you LIKE the person or team you chose to work with?

This is a home valuation generally provided for Free by most Realtors. Realtors are in the people business and often give too much away. It is more accurate than an Online Assessment. Most Agents will include detailed information on similar homes that have sold in the area in the last 3 to 6 months. Included are details of each comparable, such as how much the home listed for, any Seller Concessions and the closing sales price. Additionally, it may also include a few homes that are presently 'under contract.' These homes are considered your competition. A Realtor may also supply you with graphs depicting the value of your house over the last few years. Neighborhood walkability information, what schools are in the area. All this provides you with a value range or "Market Value" of what your house will sell for within a specified time frame in the present marketplace.

A Realtor has experience and knowledge from working in the field of real estate every day. How often to you buy and sell real estate in a year? Do you keep up with changes? Do you know why they use general forms that are specialized by State or Area? It is to protect the Seller if it's a Listing Agreement. If it's a Sales Contract it will depend on the state as to whom it most likely protect. IE: Virginia is a Buyer Beware State, meaning the contract favors the Seller. A Buyer should do their own research regarding a property and community.

Do you have a college degree of some kind? Or have you attended Trade School? If so, you know the value of paying for knowledge. You have developed skills so others may pay you a daily wage. Most Realtors in America are not paid a salary. They are paid 'commission.' This means they are paid for their knowledge only when someone who hires them reaches their goals. As a Listing Agent they need to help you market your home in order to attract a Buyer into purchasing the home and closing on that home. The Realtor is then paid at closing for their knowledge, experience and effort. If you move on to another Realtor the 1st Realtor will not receive a payment for their efforts.

Have you paid for an Appraisal on your property to be certain the price in your mind is in line with the present Marketable Value of your property? Asking a Realtor to 'preview' your property. A knowledgeable Realtor maybe willing to provide pointers on 'Curb Appeal.' They may be willing to give you pointer throughout your home that will help you sell your home quicker and for top dollar! They may provide you with a 'Comparative Market Analysis.' This is a break down of what similar homes in the area have sold for, as well as what they are presently listed for. It also goes into detail as to the overall market analysis for your neighborhood over a period of time. Generally the last 3 - 6 months. They will provide you with statistic and charts that show you data as well as insight into Schoolrating, walkability, the safety of the neighborhood, access to public transportation and shopping. Any thing significant to Buyers who will be considering purchasing your home.

Have you considered all this data when setting a price for your home? Have you considered what makes your home special? What sets it apart from the home around the corner that's listed for $10,000 less than you believe your home is worth? Are you able to look at your home objectively? Do you want to set appoints for prospective buyers to walk thru your house? Can you keep quiet when they come knocking on the door? Do you know whether they qualify to purchase your property? Have you removed valuables that a prospective buyer may be interested in taking? Have you considered why a Realtor places a lockbox on the door that allows them to track every agent that comes through the home? Does your Homeowners Insurance cover you for theft, and defects you have hidden? Do you know why Real Estate Agents have Errors & Omissions Insurance?

Does your Home Owners Policy cover accidents of someone coming through your house? That's why Realtors have Errors & Omissions! Mistakes happen, accidents happen. Years ago, I worked with a buyer. On our second meeting he had a three year old child with him. The child ran upstairs ahead of us and cut his hand on the

Mom I never left home without a first aid kit and a roll of toilet paper, and hand sanitizer in my car. The man went on and on as if the scratch were of great concern. Apparently, he forgot I mentioned he's responsible for looking after his child. I looked him in the eye as I slapped on the 1st aid cream and bandaid. "He's fine. It is a parents responsibility to hold a child's hand when touring a home they are interested in purchasing. Right?"

The man shut up quickly. It could have gone a different way. What if it had been icy and we slipped on the sidewalk when you as the Homeowner are showing someone through your home? What if you allow someone to take photos and then you're burgled?

If you have a toothache do you fill it yourself or seek the aid of a Dentist? Like a Dentist Realtor's are Licensed and Insured. Not always is the case of a Real Estate Consultant, or a Property Agent. The later two are not required to be insured as they are not licensed and neither are you.

These are just a few reasons to use a Realtor. As a Listing Agent I ask a Seller a lot of questions. I use the answers to help the Seller not only sell their home but to provide a Seller's Estimated Closing Cost Sheet for them to gage how much they may expect to walk away with. I also am able to offer other resources when needed from other professionals I have worked with in the area. I may even be able to assist with helping the seller make their move to their next location. As a Professional in the area I have knowledge and experience as well as business partners who are willing to help you through whatever issue may come up. Online resources often provide you with area professionals that pay to be on those specific sites. Word of mouth and Affiliated business is an alternative due to the fact that if my clients and referrals are not happy with the results I will replace those contacts.

Have you considered what documentations may be helpful in selling your home, as well as closing on the sale in a timely manner. I will ask you if you have a Plat or Survey. Did you pay for Title Insurance when you purchased the property? Do you have a Mortgage or Line of Credit on your property? Are there tax liens to be removed? Are you current on your mortgage? Your HOA OR POA Dues? Do you know you will need to order an HOA or POA Packet for the Buyer? How is the property ownership held in on the deed? What type of Deed do you have? What is the lot size? Dimensions?

I can assure you, after years of experience, few people think of these items as important. A Seller may or may not remember when they replaced the roof last. They may believe the hot water tank was replaced a year ago, but upon being asked for a receipt it is clear the appliance is three years old!

Did you have a water leak in the basement and paint the walls to hide the leak? By law you are required to complete a Disclosure to a potential Buyer where you make such

disclosures. In Virginia a Seller is not required to disclose known defects if working with an agent, however, a Realtor is required to disclose if they know! If you do not disclose you maybe liable. If the Realtor you hire does not see the property prior to the walls being painted and they have no knowledge of the leak they are not obliged to disclose. If you tell them, they must disclose even though you are not required to disclose when using an agent. Realize that if you had water damage of any kind and you called your Insurance Company this information will show up on 'CLUE' Report even though it did not effect your homeowners insurance premiums it may impact the buyers loan. Also, be aware that should you have a contract fall through due to a defect that defect now must become public knowledge. You can not hide it, and it may effect the value of your property.

As a Home Seller in Virginia you may say, 'It's a Buyer Beware State. Why do I need a local Realtor to sell my house?'

A few years ago I helped a Realtor sell their home and move to Kentucky. This Agent didn't believe in Home Warranties, but I encouraged him to put one in place for the new buyers anyway. After the sale he and his wife thanked me for that simple piece of advice.

Why?

As it turns out, this Agent had been in the service and raised to be a neat knick. In their efforts to clean thoroughly they had cleaned the water heater from top to bottom as that is often a place people forget and it accumulates dust. Unfortunately, he left the cleaning sponge in the drip pan when he was finished.

The new owners months later had an issue with the water heater and when they found the sponge in the drip pan they accused him of hiding a slow leak!

Rather than fight it out the Home Warranty Company stepped in and replaced the hot water heater for a $75.00 repair visit.

Money well spent!

You may be surprised to know that a Realtor does not need to know ever home and neighbor you have. They do not need to know all the gossip. They should be 'pre-viewing' homes in the area similar to your home that they see as a comparable to your home. Why? Because they are going to desire that you price your home at a Marketable price. And to know the Marketable range they need to look at the competition to understand the condition in comparison to the condition of your property.

There are at least 23 Steps a Realtor will take into consideration prior to listing a property. After listing the home the detailed work begins! There are at least 30 additional steps an agent goes through once they have a Listing Agreement in place with you. Even if you are working with an Auction Agent the steps are basically the same. Expect lots of paperwork and questions! So many disclosures come into effect when selling a property. Some Disclosures are based on location, others by State. A Realtor familiar with your neighborhood will also be familiar to what Disclosures apply to your property. You're curious as to what I mean by Disclosures. If in Virginia Beach, you have to Disclose the airplane traffic patterns near the home. If in Stafford you may need to Disclose the sound issues of Quantico and why you replace your windows every five years, are just a few

Disclosures that may cause problems when working with an 'out of town' agent or consider selling on your own. When you do not use a Licensed, Local Professional and you fail to disclose there could be consequence down the road from the new owners.

Do you have a Home Warranty? If not a Listing Agent will suggest that you put one in place while you have your property on the market. They may have given you a list of needed repairs... did you get the list completed prior to listing?

If not are you aware that not making repairs and doing a through cleaning will effect the sales price of your property? Did you work with the Realtor to 'Stage' your property? If not did you higher a Staging Professional?

Sometimes I work with Sellers that ask for advise and then do not take it. Believe me agents do not give you advise to make themselves feel good. They are doing you a service... its up to you to follow through if you want the agreed price to happen!

If I recommend you repair the pet damage and paint the front door or lower the price I mean it sincerely. Don't tell me it's done and list the house as is for the higher price and then complain when you receive poor reviews. Doing the repairs after listing is a Costly Mistake!

Has your Agent been able to answer all your questions? Were they able to give you references of local professionals to assist you in repairs, moving, storage, etc?

Now, the FUN begins!!

Chapter 1

What does a Realtor actually do for a Property Seller?

#1 *They share their experience, trusted contacts, affiliates and knowledge with the Seller for the benefit of selling a property at the best possible price based on the Seller's situation.*

#2 *They point out issues the Seller may need to address. Paper work the Seller may need to provide. And help the Seller prepare for the move in a number of ways. They have a checklist of items that need to be addressed in order for a smooth closing to take place. The checklist are based on location and property type. They often prepare a Closing Cost Sheet for the Seller* *to have an expectation of Loss or Gain on the property based on one to three sales prices.*

Utilizing a Local Realtor 8 of 10 times will bring you more money and less time in selling your property. For this reason the head of FSBO website listed with an agent years ago.

Throughout this book you will find examples of how a Realtor saved a Seller in some fashion.

It is crucial for a home seller to understand the factors that determine price when it comes to selling a home. A Realtor may list your home at a price you chose that is higher than the Realtor recommends. Why? Advertising gets listings! In the end, if you want your home to sell at a good price…. Follow directions, and don't be over zealous.

#3. A Realtor helps a Property Seller Administratively. They are the gatekeeper for the Seller. As a Listing Agent they provide and monitor the Lockbox, the Open Houses, and Broker's Opens. As well as Appraisers, Inspectors and Prospective Buyers and Buyer's Agents. They provide up to date, legally binding contracts that are specific to the area in which the property is located. (*fun fact: did you know that contracts purchased at a contractor supply house or on line may not hold up in a local court should the need arise?*)

I use to tell people who buy and sell two or three homes a year they are fine without an Agent. After one lost in court because they used a contract from a large chain handy man store I no longer say that.

A Realtor in today's Market must be somewhat Tech Savvy.

- A REALTOR can ENTER PROPERTY INTO THE MULTIPLE LISTING DATABASE for other agents in the area to see the property is available for sale. –- What? Yes, a For Sale By Owner can work with a Real Estate Broker at a flat fee to list the property in the MLS in order that other Realtors with buyers will be aware the owner will pay a Buyers agent.

- Prepare data for entry into MRIS (MLS) - agent is responsible for "quality control" and accuracy. They are suppose to verify your information with the Tax Records. A Realtor pays to participate in the Multiple Listing Service in their area.

- Proofread for listing accuracy - including proper placement in mapping

- Provide seller with broker's signed copy of the Listing Agreement

- Market the property to other agents in their office and company as a whole.

MARKETING THE PROPERTY

- Create print and Internet ads with seller's input

® Coordinate showings with owners, tenants and other REALTORS ; return all calls including weekends

- Install electronic lockbox, if authorized by owner; program the lockbox with agreed-upon showing times. Or place a combo lockbox if the owner prefers.

- Prepare mailing and contact lists

- Generate letters and combine with contact list

- Order or Create "Just Listed" postcards specific for your property

- Prepare Flyers, Internet ads, Social Media Ads, etc.

- Review comparable MLS listings regularly to ensure property remains competitive, just to mention a few things a Realtor does for the commission they hope to receive.

Is your Realtor using Video? Marketing to include cultural diverse buyers? Feature your property on their website or create a single property 'squeeze page?'

What is their marketing campaign? Do they rely solely on Zillow or Facebook and the MLS to sell your house? Or do they have an additional marketing plan in place?

Do they encourage you to allow them to do an "Open House?" Or "Broker's Open?"

I have been selling real estate in Virginia for 15 years. In all that time I have done my share of Open Houses. I have even attended classes on How to host a Successful Open House. Honestly, Open House success depends heavily on LOCATION! If you're home is unremarkable and out on a dirt road there is little expectation you will have a successful Open House. This is definitely an area where the Seller should rely on the knowledge of the professional they hired.

Let's be honest and realistic… Not every house is remarkable. If you live in a track home you can still help sell your house.

1. A deep through cleaning! (I can not stress enough the importance of Neat and Clean when it comes to attracting Top Dollar for your house!).

2. Declutter as much as possible while still occupying the house. Take out anything you can temporarily live without so that it appears larger than the home next door. (Accept that a home in need of work or very cluttered is not going to sell for as much as a home in top shape that is tidy and clean!!).

If affordable paint the master bedroom ceiling the same color as the walls… preferably a lavender or dove gray. These colors enlarge a room, as does the uniform coloring.

Alternatively option… dress up the main hall bathroom with fun colors! Dare to paint the walls Orange or bright Green with a bright fish shower curtain. Remove shampoos, lotions, knick knacks from the counter. They can neatly remain in shower or tub, But NOT ON THE COUNTER AROUND THE SINK. You want everything clean and neat!

Stop watching DYI shows, or Flip this House! They are a total distraction when attempting to sell your own property! **Remember:** for every hour you saw on TV there were countless hours off film for *those people to pull every thing together with seeming,'ease.' Its Reality TV, that doesn't make it Live TV.*

Recently:

I was chatting with a local antiques dealer He confessed that last year he had an epiphany!

He sold his 4800 square foot home, Auctioned off a Huge amount of stuff and built a Tiny Home on 10 acres.

His new home sits over top a two car garage. He has a four car detached garage he uses to store his antiques business and has found a great deal of joy in living in less clutter.

It has given him a sense of freedom!

Knowing your Motivation for a move makes the move go smoother!

A move requires you to Let Go!

In today's internet world do you need a local Realtor to help you sell your house or property?

As a Licensed Professional of course my response is, 'YES!'

Please allow me to expound on ones need for a professional in a day and age when you can sell your house on line.

Honestly, for years I would tell people who were working with a New Construction, 'You know what you want. You have a professional developer you don't need me.'

WRONG!!!! Why? You ask.

Why Indeed? Perhaps it's because Developers build in the cost of working with a licensed professional whether you have one or not.

Developers up sell on the finishing touches, ie: counter tops, basements, carpets, cabinets, etc. They talk fast and before you know it you have agreed to spend $100,000 more than you expected! You may not even realize how much you're over budget because they work on monthly payments. They use the present tax rate, not what the rate will be with a house on the property! All is justifiable to a Developers sales force. They do not represent your interest, they represent the developer... do not mistake the difference!

When I work with a Buyer on new construction its my job to keep them constantly aware of what they are buying, including up sell items and material. A Developer may charge $225 - $300 per additional out let you desire to be in a room. They may not charge anything to place their allotted outlet in a specific place or way... that's where an experienced professional comes in handy. I have saved people $50,000 by negotiating price and working with my buyers as to the best time to purchase new construction. I was even able to get a jilted bridegroom out of a purchase because I know enough to know when something doesn't look right or consistent. That's when I seek expert advise and in this case it was enough to get a release of the deposit for my client. Do you pay a mechanic to tune up your car? Or

do you do it yourself? When working as a Buyer's Agent think of me as a Buyer's mechanic for new construction.

But this is information for another book! **The buyer's handbook!**

Back to the basics of Selling your Property!!

So, you have decided to sell your house, or some other piece of property. Now, you need to consider: Time, Effort, and Investment! Why are these important? I will show you.

80% of Selling your home is how motivated are you to sell? Are you willing to do whatever it takes to prepare your home for the market? Your willingness will effect the sales price of the home.

Once a property is listed expect to adjust to the changes in your day to day life. The house needs to be clean... that includes walls, doors, floors, sinks, toilets, etc. Beds need to be made, laundry done. The lawn mowed, garbage not left to pile up! Are you prepared to deal with this daily? Expect phone calls from buyers-agents, from the general public that may wish to rent rather than buy. Buyers-Agents will want to set appointments. People may simply come and knock on the door to see the home.

Realize children and pets may be a distraction for a potential buyer. You should make arrangements for your children to be elsewhere and pets crated or kenneled outside. Many more people will schedule a showing than will actually purchase the home. Many buyers agents provide a list of homes for their clients to consider without having a clear picture of what the buyer wants. Since a showing can take up to two to three hours of your time, finding an interested buyer is what matters to you! This is not a perfect world, not all calls will lead to serious buyers. As I said, some people will come calling to see if you will rent the home instead of selling.

Some agents do not ask if their client has been pre-approved, so they may not qualify for your property. Others, are just beginning the process and want to see your house because it appeals to them on some level.

By understanding your local market value you will see why its important to focus on your properties best features. Why presentation goes a long way and some great strategies to sell your property in a timely fashion!

Chapter 2

What is the 80/20 rule in marketing?
And Why should I care?

   The **80/20 rule**, also known as the Pareto Principle, is attributed to
the Italian economist, Vilfredo Pareto. Applying it to the business world,
the **80/20 rule** suggests that 80% of your company sales come from
20% of your customers.
   This breaks down to 80% of all sales comes from 20% of buyers.
What this means to you is that your Realtor is advertising in a variety of
ways because they know these averages. They know where the
majority of their sales come from in their market. That's why they
advertise geographically, or target a certain income bracket.
Depending on the property they may advertise to a certain niche
group... ie: hunters, or horsemen, etc.
   How does this Principle apply to your specific property? Remember
when I said: Focus on the Best Features of your property? Consider
this: roughly 20% of your properties features will be 80% of the reason
it sells.

> A Seller's Story
> When Ken & Shanda listed their home on 20 acres they needed
> a buyer who desired a dirt road, privacy and wanted to be in
> control of their water and septic system.
> A 10 year old home with some wear and tear offered some
> amazing features, like the custom made dining area with a see
> thru fireplace, and open balcony above.
> The Buyers looked at a similarly sized home 10 miles closer to
> the Metropolitan DC area with similar features. But it was in an
> HOA, with less land.
> What 20% of this home out weighted the shorter distance to
> DC?   The Buyers loved the privacy 25 acres offered. They loved
> the way the home was laid out to provide room for growth or for
> an Air B&B opportunity.

The 80/20 Rules works in many aspects of our lives.
20% of the Causes equal 80% of the Outcomes.
Examples:

   *. 80% of your work comes from 20% of your effort
   *. As stated previously, 80% of a businesses sales are derived from
20% of their customers
   *. 80% of your value to your employer is from 20% of your work.

Why should this rule apply to you?

When we use the 80/20 rule to home sales we STOP selling the whole house! What do you Love most about this property? What motivates you will motivate others! Now, highlight the 20% of your property's features that make it special. The other 80% matters, so keep it nice, but it is not the 'draw.'

By focusing on what's uniques about your home you will grab the attention of buyers.

Consider, an out-of-town prospect with no specific requirements popped into my office in Southpoint Plaza to see what was available in the area. Two older men. One proceeded to tell me he had been to another real estate office around the corner where he was not treated with the respect and courteous he had expected. I brought him back into my office and we chatted. He planned to pay cash for a home for him and some of his employees as they had a two year job in the area. He provided me with the name of his banker and he had the documentation providing he had funds to look for a very nice home.

We scrolled through a few homes for sale in the area. I scheduled appointments for the next day. As we looked they made it clear what they liked and didn't like about the homes. They were accustom to finished garages and basements, all the homes we looked at were unfinished. They felt each home was overpriced by 20 to 30%. It began to pour rain.

Finally, we reached the last house late in the day. It was a large, colonial like the other six homes we had looked at. We walked in the living room with an open ceiling and high windows on either side of the stone fireplace that let in the light! Finally, we had a home of interest to the two men. The basement had two sump pumps and seemed to have a water issue based on the location. They were not deterred, the garage was oversized and finished!

Amazingly, they had found a home and they found it priced well for the area. He was done, the decision was made!
The home backed to the power line and they both found that appealing as it gave them assurance there would be no more building

The 80/20 Rule Applies to Home Sales

Last year I had a repeat client desire to move to a larger home. We spent a couple of days looking at similar homes. The husband repeatedly wanted to offer 10% to 20% less than asking in a competitive market. Needless to say, we were continually denied. Finally, we went to a basic, brick colonial in a good location. There was plenty of parking.

What set this home apart from all the others? What caused this couple to simply go with close to asking price?

It sat in a cul de sac with a foot trail into the woods! It was back into an established neighborhood, no sound of traffic, with the trees behind them. No neighbors to look into their yard from that perspective. The path provided further distance from the neighbors than any of the other homes had offered. They were so taken with the patio and the view the rest of the home didn't matter

The home buyer based his purchase right there on the deck, and view of peace and quiet he would have.

behind them. This was the place for them. 80% of the homes had similar space and lay-outs. They had not truly been interested until we walked in the last house. This place had all the features they were interested in, and it wasn't the large, airy kitchen, or the bedrooms that sold the house. It was the great room and the wide open view out back. The view gave them a sense of space they were both accustom to, and that is what they bought.

In retrospect, this buyer based his decision to buy on the windows and the view. Just 20% of the home's features motivated them to make a cash offer of just 3% below asking price. Such is the power of the 80/20 rule.

There are times when the 80/20 rule helps people purchase sight unseen. There are some that will purchase from afar by relying on their agent to preview the home for them

based on the specifics they have provided their agent. I have known agents that video specific features of homes to find one that will satisfy the needs of out of town buyers.

When a buyer is in another country and needs a home ready when he arrives relies on the eyes of the Realtor he hires to help him find the 20% of a home that interest him most. In a Buyer's Market there is the motivation of fear someone else will purchase the home before he has a moment to consider it. Such a buyer was able to close in 45 days from the day the agent pre-viewed the home.

The irony, this home had been floundering on the market for almost eight months. The Seller's had already moved to a new location and were becoming worried it was not priced well. The 80/20 rule holds true repeatedly.

How can this rule be applied to your house? How can you leverage this knowledge and find the unique selling point of your property? Sit for a moment and try to remember; what was your favorite thing about your home when you purchased it or had it built? Where do you spend most of your time now? Those are most likely the same features that will bring another person to purchase the house as well. Focus on making those features stand out and your house will sell for close to or at the selling price.

Shift away from all the fluff, or all that needs to be done. Focus on the main draw of the property as a whole and sell just that 20% and you will find your home is very desirable.

Keep in mind: Buyers seek out Unique Features

What sets your home apart from all your neighbors homes? What is unique to yours from the other homes on the market? When you focus your efforts on those features you will attract interested buyers who are willing and able to pay the asking price.

Let's consider a few Unique Features to consider

Even track homes have a unique feature to set it apart from the neighbors. Here are a few features to consider, but keep in mind they are not absolute.

- ✦ **Hilltop views** provide an excellent defining feature that will be unique to each home based on the vantage point, and views of the surrounding area.
- ✦ **Does your house look out over an open field with views of wildlife?** This is often a feature people find attractive.
- ✦ **Your house may have an amazing view of the sunset.** This is another incredible feature of interest to potential buyers
- ✦ **Patios are another positive feature.** Is yours bigger than other patios? Or perhaps you have one where others do not. This becomes a vital feature to help sell your house.
- ✦ **LOCATION is an important factor in selling a house!** If your house is on a Cul-de-sac or a its a corner lot, make the most of this information when marketing the property. Buyers will pay more for a End-Unit Townhome than for an Interior townhome in the same complex. Why? Because the End-Unit tends to have a yard the other properties did not have. The End-Units generally sell for more and quicker than other units in the same complex because of the yard.

Another homeowner in the same Townhouse Complex may also sell for more than
other interior properties because it offers a special feature. Say it backs to a lake,

stream or golf course. These features will help you sell your
townhome quickly
        and at a great price.

◆   **You might have a private location.** Consider; is your lot partially concealed by trees? Do you have a fenced in yard? Do you have an empty lot next door? Do you have private parking? These are things to consider as features when marketing your property.

◆ **Is your backyard larger than the neighbors?** If so, you have a special selling point that is to your advantage. Just as a shady backyard may draw some and scare away others. I have meant a number of people over the years that have a concern of trees close to the house, or too many in the backyard. It is a great feature to those that enjoy shade. It may be a deterrent to those that enjoy sunbathing in the privacy of their backyard.

◆ **A number of years ago there was a house in Falmouth that didn't sell.** It was in a great neighborhood, had an amazing basement. But the basement didn't have a walk out. A more seasoned agent suggested adding a rear entrance to the basement. He arranged for contractor and engineer to look at the home and provide estimates. The homeowners realized they could add a basement entrance for less than $10,000. This addition brought them an increased sales price of $20,000 and a fast closing!

Keep in mind... when you look for the 20% Difference and Market those Features you will see Results!

There is proof the 80/20 rule works time and again. The more you apply this simple rule the less time you will waste showing your home to uninterested prospective buyers. Instead, you will be sought out by motivated buyers ready to purchase.

Wouldn't it be great to avoid low ball offers from investors looking to profit at your expense? Isn't it better not to have many showings, but the ones you have are from qualified, serious buyers?

Now, take the time to consider the best features of your house and property. How can a Realtor help you highlight that one feature that will make your house attractive and unique? Look at the neighbors homes, how does your house stand out?? Do you have an amazing, lush green, perfectly manicure lawn? Does your have a view of a lake or river? Do you offer more privacy? Whatever that feature is, focus on that being the main feature of the house. Highlight it in every way. Make sure that feature shines!

4
Curb Appeal

According to recent statistics 80% of todays home buyers begin looking online 12 - 18 months before they begin physically touring properties. Whether a home buyer is shopping online or driving by they will decide in a glance as to whether or not your property has any interest for them. A few years ago people from my church asked me to help them find a new home. They were interested in several different areas and we scheduled several days to look at property in each given area. One area was too rural for the wife. There were three homes she would not even get out of the car to go into look at. She had liked them well enough online, but had not realized the Location was totally unsuitable for her. That First Impression is sometimes all you get. Curb appeal is crucial to maintaining interest in your house. You want to be inviting, and appealing from the road. An appealing photo of the curb view of your house may be far more attractive to a potential buyer than the written description.

When you drive around your neighborhood, and the surrounding area what do you find appealing of other homes? Is it the homes with clean yards? Well manicured lawns, do you smell the fresh cut grass? Or are they overgrown with abandoned cars off to the side? Keep in mind, the outside appearance of your property is an invitation to come or not come inside.

Make each Potential Home Buyer feel the warmth your home offers. Let them be drawn in by a sense of 'Welcome,' as they drive by. Be sure you have the fresh cut lawn, the trimmed trees and hedges. A clean, neat yard, porch or walkway. Power wash the exterior to give it that clean, fresh feel. Paint the front door a clean lacquer coat so it doesn't look weathered. The outward appearance sets the stage for the inside. Make it as appealing as possible. Give the impression it has been well maintained over the years.

The Importance of curb appeal is like a well wrapped gift. The box may be empty inside, but you choose it because it's so well wrapped. When a potential buyer drives up to your house they take inventory of what they see. If you want top-dollar for your property expect the buyer to be looking for 'move-in-ready.' If they see things needing attention on the outside they will be looking closer to the inside. Simply weeding the flower beds, trimming the hedges and washing the windows you improve the appearance of your home with a bit of effort and not a lot of cost.

Look for Low-cost investments like a through, deep cleaning inside and out. Consider the importance of Power-washing the house, and sidewalk and any other concrete nearby.

Power washing can really brighten up the appearance of the house and the concrete around it. It pays to hire a professional to power wash even though it seems simple. Siding has 'weep holes' and if power washing is not done correctly you could allow moist to get in between the siding and installation of the house and cause mold to grow. You do not want that issue. Paint the trim, add some landscaping, or flowers. Color is a great way to brighten the outside of a house. I have even seen people put out wax flowers in cold weather to brighten the appeal of the home. I am not convinced that silk or wax flowers along the walk way will help sell a house. Remember: your goal is to get more money for your house in a timely fashion. Honestly, if a home is in need of repair expect to sell it for below market value.

If your yard is unkempt or your house has peeling paint, or there is a sense its out dated Home Buyers may drive by without wanting to go inside. They may cancel from the roadside.

If you had an agent come out to pre-list the house they most likely gave you a list of repair considerations. Take serious heed as these items will effect the price. Are you will to put in the effort to do the work?

Ask yourself:
❉ Are the shrubs, trees, flower gardens, etc. tidy?
❉ Is there trash and general debris that needs cleaned up?

✳ Is the driveway and walk-way in good shape?
✳ Do the outside lights, garage door, and porch rails work properly?
✳ Could the outdoor features use new cushions or a new coat of paint?

Are you willing to make these necessary improvements to update the exterior of your property? Do you see how making the outside inviting will bring more prospective buyers into your house? How easy small improvements will make a better sale?

Anyone can list a house for sale. Not everyone will sell their home quickly for a good price. The more curb appeal you have the greater the profit.

Most homes have an ability to Create a Grand Entrance

A Front Door is *Important!* It makes a lasting impression, just as the curb appeal. You want to give the impression of safety and security when they open the door.

I recently listed a rental property, the door knob gave me a bit of trouble to open. The clients toured the home and liked it until we went to leave and the door knob literally came off in my hand! We had to go out through the garage. They did not rent the house, needless to say!

Suffice to say a flimsy lock or handle on the front door will make prospective home buyers hesitant, and they may not even know why. Security is very important to a home buyer.

Keep in mind the front door is a focal point. Make it impressive! Recently, I had a couple with a scratched up front door. They had two large dogs. Initially, the husband did not see a
need to repair and paint the front door. They were sure the positive aspects of the home would out weigh the minor repairs needed. When the property didn't sell as timely as they liked he finally agreed to the minor repairs. They ended up with multiple offers on the home.

So, lesson learned... make the Front door impressive! Look at it as if from a buyers perspective. Is the door faded? Flaky or peeling?

Could it use a fresh coat of paint? Be sure to choose a paint that complements the color of your home.

Have you considered replacing an old wooden door with a steel entry door? Do you know the cost is worth it based on a 91% return on investment!

What is curb appeal? How does one create it?

* Symmetry appeals to the eye, and is rather simple to accomplish. Sit back and really look at your yard. Is the landscape lopsided or unevenly trimmed? This is distracting to the overall curb appeal.
* What is the overall appearance of your home? Is there balance? Does it flow?
* If you have a mailbox, make certain it is sturdy and properly placed and matches the overall appearance of your house.
* A simple and often overlooked outside touch is lighting. Outdoor lighting adds to your landscaping. I had a couple that fell in love with the small outdoor lights strung around the patio. So much so, they actually had me make them a part of the sale! Keep in mind lighting is not just perceived as beauty, it is also perceived as a safety feature.
* We've all seen how flower boxes can add a lovely splash of color. Raised gardens or well placed flower beds are another way to enhance the exterior appearance of your house.
* Spruce up the landscaping surrounding your house. Be sure to weed the gardens and add fresh mulch for a fresh, appealing look.
* Would your home pop by simply adding a bit of crown molding at the top of the walls or a chair rail. Fresh paint for the trim of doorways and windows.
* Be sure to inspect the shutters and trim. A good, fresh coat of paint will make them more attractive. Inspect the fence, gates, etc. Be sure the gates and doors all work well.
* Clean downspouts and gutters. Be sure to clean the gutters! You need to be certain your home doesn't appear neglected.
* Make sure the walkways to your front door is easy to approach. Clear away hoses, and trim back landscaping. You want to be sure all is inviting.

* If your railings look weathered are you willing to apply a fresh coat of stain?
* The overall Appearance of your home will make a difference on the sale price. Every effort you take is of value to you overall. When you look at the exterior paint is good, make sure your doors and window trim are too. Is well worth the cost to make these little upgrades. They will add exponentially to the overall look and feel of your house.
* Power washing the house, the walkways, and driveway can be almost as effective as repainting if done well.
* Adding some stones along the walk may go a long way.
* Add a 'smart' doorbell. Invest approximately $200 for a doorbell with a camera and speaker will go along way with todays home shoppers.

Curb appeal is one of the most important elements in selling your home quickly and successfully. You can create interest in your home quickly and successfully. You can create interest in your home before buyers even step out of the car, no matter how uninterested they might have been initially. Learn about strategic interior staging in the upcoming chapters.

Realize the power of photography when it comes to marketing your house. Consider where to spend and where to save. Commit your time and effort to update and make as many improvements and updates as possible. Each improvement you make will help with your houses appraisal and each prospective buyers viewing.

5

Staging with Purpose

Staging is effective in any market. No matter what type of home is being listed. Professional staging will help sell a home quickly and for more money.

What is Staging? This is the act of sprucing up a home and make it as visually appealing as possible. A Stager often utilizes furnishings in the home by reorganizing them to bring out the best features of the house. Its amazing how a good eye can freshen up a house.

Selling a house in a timely fashion in today's competitive market takes you working hand in hand with your Realtor. It requires hard work and dedication. If you are a motivated seller, you will want to Create an eye-appealing home and property. Utilize some simple staging techniques most Realtors are familiar with. You want just one potential buyer to envision themselves living in this house! That's the best investment of your time and effort!

What will Staging do for me?

◆ This is a Great way to SET your home apart from the competition
◆ Looking to attract top $$? Take a moment to accomplish this step
◆ Visuals are a great 'edge' over the competition.

If you're like most Americans you do not keep your home showroom neat. It's very helpful to step back and let someone else come in and move things around or give you pointers on how to bring out the best features of each room so that a potential buyer may envision themselves and their belongings in your space.

Staging is Powerful when selling a home. Do you consider just how much?

Consider the simple facts that speak for themselves. Coldwell Banker and the National Association of Realtors conducted a survey.

- ✦ Staged homes on average spent 50% less time on the market that other homes.

- ✦ Staged homes overall sell for 6% above the asking price

- ✦ Consider: a Staging Investment of 1% to 3% of asking price generates a return on investment between 8% and 10% - is it worth it to you?

- ✦ Keep in mind, you only get one shot at a "FIRST IMPRESSION." That's why homes staged prior to Listing on average sold 79% faster than homes staged after listing.

A Realtor for United Country spent time with the CEO, Dan Duffy, for the show 'Under Cover Boss' sharing the secret strategy of staging. Dan maybe the CEO, but he will be the first to admit his is not a Realtor or an Auctioneer. His gift is not in selling real estate. He is very talented at building businesses and helping others develop their passions. Dan listened and learned something he had never considered before. He spent time in a bedroom implementing the techniques shared by the agent. Utilize items thorough out the home if necessary to pull a room together in a way that makes it more inviting. Be sure any photos or knick knacks used flow and match the setting in the room. Dan realized in that afternoon that being a Real Estate Professional was far more than he had initially imagined. These professionals are often underrated for their knowledge, psychological understanding of people overall and the situations they face daily.

A Realtor is constantly changing their hat to meet the need of their clients and market themselves to the public at large. All while still taking a moment to consider what are the best options with what they have to work with.

The better a home is staged the better it sells, and the more commission a Realtor will get for their efforts. Conversely, even when an excellent effort is put forth and every thing is by the book there is no guarantee that every home will sell. That Agent has put in tremendous time and effort and the listing expired. The agent receives no compensation for their effort.

After staging there is a moment when an agent simply must, 'hold their breath.' They have worked with the Seller to bring the home in shape as much as the seller was willing to do. The price is set, other similar homes may come on the market and list
for less in an effort to sell quickly. At this point all an agent can do is A. Suggest the seller lower their price to match the competition. Or B. Hold steady and have faith!
When Seller 'B' is my client we stand firm. I pray a lot and assure them, 'we only need one Buyer to fall in love.'

It's a great experience to work with a Seller that listens to my suggestions and desires to really work with me to help sell their property. I have a beautiful couple at the present that has fallen on some tight times. They still live comfortable and walk around each day with a ready smile, but they truly 'need' to sell their present home
and simplify a bit.
These gracious lady called me one day and asked, "T.C. do you have a sewing machine?"
"Yes, but the last time I used it I had to have my son show me how to thread the bobbin." I answered honestly.
"Oh. No worries, I'm going to learn to sew." She decided right there over the phone. A few weeks later she called to invite me over...
Wow! She had purchased new fabric and form for their lounge furniture on the patio. It LOOKED AMAZING! I felt like I

walked into a photo from Southern Living Magazine! Just Beautiful!

A few days later we received a Showing Request and that was the day the home was SOLD!!

What can I say? Staging works!

I have a high end listing that was previously in the hands of another Realtor. Initially, she staged the home, arranged for high end photos to betaken. She received a contract close to the $1,200,000.00 asking price! The Sellers accepted. Even though the Buyers were from another country the earnest money deposit was held by their agents firm. The closing date came and went, the out of country buyer never appeared. The Earnest Money Deposit turned out to be non-existent. The Seller's called me. I suggested they continue to work with the agent to obtain another buyer. A second buyer stepped forward, however, due to unforeseen issues of the Buyers their financing fell through.

Time dragged on and the Sellers had to go. Now, the home was empty, someone came and removed many of the kitchen appliances. They called me in again. This time I did accept the listing. We cleaned up what we could. I had photos from years before and focused on some of the amazing features of the home and land. Even without all the kitchen appliances and no furniture I listed and sold the home for $830,000.00 within 45 days of getting the listing. Why do I use this seemingly terrible example?

Two fold: The Staging efforts of the firth Agent Brough actually multiple buyers to the property. Buyer one fell through. A second buyer came right behind them but lost their financing. That was not for lack of effort on the part of the listing agent, or the property. I am using this example because here we have the EXACT same house in different stages selling for substantially different prices. Staging brought 2 buyers at $1,200,000.00 in an area where the best expected price was $649,000.00 for that property. My appraiser girlfriend, Lisa Hockman, toured the house and was not certain she would be able to appraiser it for $1,200,000 because there were simply no comparables.

I came into a situation where the home was much like other homes in the area. The owners had been transferred out of the area. Sometimes, people take the kitchen appliances with them. For all any prospective buyers knew that was the case here in my listing of $830,000 I had photos of a complete kitchen as it had been. But the kitchen was not the best feature of this home, it was just a focal point of the home. By focusing on the best features of the property as a whole I received multiple offers on the home and the Sellers accepted one for $830,000.00.

Without staging I was able to attract multiple offers for more than those around the property for the simple fact that this was an unusual property for the area. Without staging I had the same home as previously listed for $1,200,000.00 sell for $830,000.00. The biggest difference was STAGING.

Is it worth the initial investment to you to take a moment and a small investment of the value of your property to stage it for the best possible price?

What is the Psyche of a Buyer?

I am not a Psychologist, however, I am a trained Licensed Professional Realtor who has worked with both Buyers and Sellers for many years. Most home shoppers are looking for a home that represents a fresh start. A status of, 'who they are.' If they walk into your house and envision themselves living there it is far easier to sell. This is why 80% of Home Buyers

Shop Online today before ever calling a Realtor or letting anyone know they are considering making a move in this direction. Photos of 20% of your property focusing on your very best features is like 'Curb Appeal' online. A Buyer's eyes are drawn to the photographs. They seek out space, and light depicted in a snapshot. Are there any unique features mentioned in the remarks, or captured in a photo that makes your property special? A clean, tidy room suggests to a potential buyer, this place is easy to maintain. This is why paint, carpet and updated fixtures go a long way in selling a house! Eliminating stained carpet, popcorn ceilings and bold, yellowed wallpaper improves the salability of your house by 75%. It doesn't need to be the most expensive fixture Lowe's or Home Depot has to offer, it simply needs to be update, and a style to match the home. The home needs to be clean, and tidy and bright! Light sells homes! A Light, Airy Atmosphere is pleasant to most people and they will seek out and buy a home that has those touches.

This step is so important that today you can find Professional Stagers in most towns. Or you can find plenty of books available today on Home Staging in stores and libraries. Realtors have collected their knowledge from years of experience and produced books to share pointers with others. Additionally, you can find lots of Interior Designs in magazines. These books whether by Realtors or Interior Designers quite often are packed with tips and examples listed as 'case studies.'

When I was in my twenties, my Aunt Junia showed me the importance of staging at a yard sale. She was not a sales person by trade, she was a high school French Teacher. But she grew up on a farm and sold eggs to pay her way through Middlebury College in Vermont. Junia knew the art of persuasion. She decided to have a yard sale and asked for my assistance.

I set it all up neatly in the yard and posted big signs. There was very little interest, even though we were on a main road. Aunt Junia came by a few hours into the sale. It was not going well until she spread out several old colorful flour sacks on the hillside of the lawn. She moved things about and made the neatly stacked clothes messy. People began to stop. People raved at finding the old flour sacks. So many people stopped to look at them and reminisce about the clothes their Mothers had made from those types of flour sacks. They shook their heads in dismay that the sacks were not made as nicely today as they had been back then. We began selling loads of things! Junia smiled and winked at me before going on her way. She showed me how to make a connection with the passer bye along the road.

Food for thought: A big part of selling is knowing how to place items in an appealing arrangement. Make a connection with the prospective buyer with out door and indoor staging. It goes a long way.

Flash forward to 2004 when I met Broker Judy Johnson. She believed every home would benefit from staging, so much so, she would ask a Seller if they minded if she rearranged a few rooms for photos and then she would put things back. Rarely did anyone turn her down from her request. Most often they would tell us we could leave things as we rearranged them. Why did Judy do such things? She knew the power of Staging! By moving things around and removing a few pieces from a room she could make it seem bigger or brighter for photos. She had a good camera and expected every agent to have a good camera as well. Why? Because as you may have heard…. **A Picture States a Thousand Words!** Therefore, a top quality photo will help sell any home. Judy was right, a good camera can compensate for low light and other minor issues. The result would be a good sale.

Today, we have DYI TV. Chances are that you, dear reader, have watched on of the many shows available on the importance of "Staging." I watched one in the doctors office that recorded prospective buyers touring a home prior to staging and then again after staging. This show had invited back the same buyers for a second look. Each time the response was the same. They found the home far more appealing after it was staged. It makes a huge difference in purchase price and time of sale.

A few years ago, I had a single lady looking for a townhome in a particular area in Fredericksburg. She wanted to live closer to her Mother and sister. We looked for a home in a neighborhood where most of the townhomes were all set up the same. They were either two bedroom or three bedrooms. She clearly wanted a two bedroom townhome. I was amazed she chose the most expensive townhome in the neighborhood! I encouraged her to offer much less than the list price as the home was over priced for the neighborhood. She finally agreed to offer half way between the average and the list price. The owner countered and a price was eventually agreed to just shy of the asking price. I questioned whether this townhome would even appraised at $130,000 in 2009 that was high for a two bedroom townhome in Bragg Hill. At that time the average 2 bedroom townhome in that neighborhood sold for between $90,000 and $110,000. It did appraise for the $130,000 sales price and we closed on this home to the great pleasure of my client and much to my surprise!

The only difference between this townhome and those comparable that had sold before it and those on the market we had also toured at the time... this home was staged from top to bottom. A new sliding glass door, new stainless steel appliances in the kitchen where the competition all had old white appliances. A fenced in square of a backyard. A new stackable washer and drier, which she liked as it was a great space saver. All the trim was painted dove gray rather than the standard white or black. New pale gray carpet upstairs in the bedrooms and hall and coming down the stairs. All the others had the standard builder grade beige carpet.

This home was staged with tasteful framed prints on the walls, complimentary furniture to bring out the gray trim. Flower pots on either side of the little walk up to the house. The door was painted a lacquered red with black shutters and door trim the red really popped. It was a cute and cozy townhome. Very inviting and definitely appealing to my buyer. A few fresh touches made this home 'Move-in' Ready.

Flash forward to just two years ago, I had an investor looking to purchase a few homes in the same neighborhood. We went to see the most highest priced home in the neighborhood out of curiosity. This home staged, but not well. There was curb appeal that clearly were an attempt to cover up the issue that roots were tearing up the foundation. We entered the front door to see cockroaches scurrying away from us. Yuck! We went into the kitchen and out the backdoor. Someone had remodeled poorly to use the small attached storage room as part of the house. Sadly, they left a gap at the top of the remodel which would allow the cold of the outside directly into the kitchen! Upstairs, it was clear the roof leaked and they had painted over stains in an active leak which caused the ceiling to bubble. The more we saw the closer the investor looked for more issues. Not only was this townhome overpriced it had been very poorly staged.

Note to self: If you are going to invest in Staging a Home, take care of obvious issues that will effect the price of a property. And secondly, spend the money wisely to include realizing what you are not able to do well yourself. By that townhome sitting on the market to long at the wrong price it only hurt the Seller and their interest. They would have been better for that seller to have invested on repair to the roof and the shed and kitchen pantry. Additionally, they would greatly benefit from hiring a professional to fumigate to be rid of the cockroaches. Poor staging does not benefit anyone and rarely fools the potential buyers.

If you have a property in need of repair fear not! Choose a few less expensive repairs that you can tackle and invest in making those repairs. Still clean the house up! A tidy house is far more inviting than one that is cluttered and messy. A shabby home in spit spot shape will still sell for more than that of a cluttered home!

In 2010 I listed a home in Stafford, Virginia. Upon my initial interview there were pathways through the house. All was neat and clean, the lady just had too much stuff! Additionally, there were some electrical issues upstairs. She said she had lived with them for several years and was not concerned.

I suggested she rent a P.O.D. and empty the house as much as possible. She mentioned her children had already made the same suggestion. She liked having lots of her 'things' around her, but she agreed to rent the P.O.D. and begin the process of emptying out 27 years of living. A few weeks later she phoned to say she was ready to have me back for a pre-listing appointment.

Wow, what a difference as we walked through the home! So much space! A transformation!

She and I moved a few pieces of furniture about for better placement and lighting and I began taking initial photos.

The home was under contract within two weeks of listing. The buyer's home inspector noted the electrical issues and the Seller refused to make repairs. The buyers desired the home and accepted it 'as is.' They closed on a full price offer. My Seller was pleased and asked me to help her find and buy a smaller home with the proceeds.

When you have provided a valuable service for a client and you keep in touch with them you will often receive repeat business as well as referrals from those clients. It has been the way experienced Realtors have stayed in business for ages. We are now in a season of business when we are told Referrals are not the way to continue working. I strongly disagree. Yes, it has become easier to purchase a home on line in our Global Society, however, I firmly believe there is still a place for Realtors. There is value in using a Knowledgeable Experts that looks out for your best interest while you're looking for the best choices of selling a home and moving. As a Seller you do not have the same prospective of your property as a Buyer or a Realtor, or an Appraiser. Additionally, you may not have the same negotiation stills as a Realtor.

Remember: a big part of a Realtor's job is to negotiate the best price for their client. The second job of a Listing Agent is to Market your home for sale in a variety of ways. Depending on Location the Marketing may vary. Marketing is area specific. Just as photos are unique depending on the category and location.

Recently, my husband and I attended Public School Band Competition. Our Fifth Grade Band took 1st Place. Not because our band was the best in their category. It turned out they took 1st Place because they were the only 5th Grade Band that participated in this particular competition. This was a Tri-State competition, and no other school had bothered to participate with their students. Another school took First Place in 6th Grade Choir. Again, they were the only 6th Grade Choir. No Competition puts you in First Place Automatically. When you work with an experienced agent to List your home and you follow their Step by Step Advice you are like these students... You put yourself in First Place because with that Realtors Knowledge of the Market you have No Competition!

The advantage to working with me. I have loved architecture since the six grade when a class field trip to look at various Collum designs opened my eyes to a world I had never noticed before! I have traveled all over the country and the world. My Father became a coal miner at the age of 12 out of necessity. He enlisted in the US ARMY to serve his country and instilled in each of us a desire for a better life. Because of my upbringing, I have had the benefit of living in a number of states and communities. I have toured thousands of homes in my career. Both large, high end homes and small or low end homes. I have walked thousands of acres of land. I have found financing for strip malls, tenants for apartments as well as business buildings. I have seen what sells in a variety of markets over a span of thirty plus years. And I have seen what doesn't sell. Do you believe I may have some knowledge that I can share with you?

Case in Point:

Some years ago I took a listing that had been a rental where the tenants had stopped paying and had to be evicted. It was in a sad state, the tenants had stayed in the home without electricity for a period of time. They had not been the neatest of people. They had left a lot of 'stuff' behind.

At the time I worked in an office that offered weekly tours. I had taken this listing, but we had not yet listed it for sale as it needed work. I put the home on the tour to get feed back from other agents on how best to use the little funds the seller had.

Mind you, the house SMELLED DREADFUL from rotten food and loads of Trash!

One of the Associate Brokers deemed this the 'Smelly House.' She flat out told me 'IT is over priced and will never sell at that price.'

I thanked her and believed it was priced under market value to accommodate for the required repairs. I was looking for ideas to enhance this home in order to get that low price without spending a fortune.

I called the 'Salvation Army to donate the furniture. They would not come to pick it up as it was worn, and not worth their time. So, I helped the owner with a "Yard Sale." We arranged two weekends and with the help of my children we pulled out stuff to put on the lawn for sale. The owner gave my children the proceeds of the yard sale for their efforts.

The owner paid for the removal of a broken refrigerator and months of trash to be removed from the basement. The tenants had painted part of the wall in the foyer a different color. As this was a split foyer that was the first thing you saw when you walked in the front door. There was no electricity or running water in this place and the owner was not going to put any on to assist in the sale for fear of squatters.

I cleaned the kitchen to some degree as there was no electricity or water. Clorox Wipes were not readily available at this time. I relied on a Mr. Clean sponge and a jug of water in the sink. I used a wet/dry mop on the floor for a cursory going over at best. While cleaning I discovered the Baker's Rack in the corner was not bolted in place, it was simply attached with grease build-up and dirt! Removing that rack really opened up the kitchen! Removing the trash and broken refrigerator and purchasing some 'odor eaters' diminished the smell of the place.

As the items were removed from the home it became apparent this was once a lovely split foyer home with a wonderful backyard that was simply overgrown! Both the house and yard needed work! We call that TLC, and the majority would be placed on the new owner.

Once these simple efforts were complete I composed a letter I sent out to all the investors in the area as well as agents I knew had investors or invested themselves. We had multiple offers on this home and it sold above list the list price of $130,000 due to my joint effort with the owner.

Point: Utilizing the aid of a Realtor is not simple to negotiate contracts or provide a Market Analysis. This Owner used my expertise, as well as knowledge of the market, and investors in the market, and asked for some of my additional time and effort. When talking to other agents this is all part of the
services we provide our clients on a daily bases without out publishing these facts regularly. A Realtor is in the Service Industry as well as the Marketing Industry and the Sales Industry. We wear many hats gladly!

As indicated in the above Case, a little Staging and Effort can go a long way in any market with any house!

Neutralize to catch the eye!

So often I walk into 'cookie cutter' styled homes all with 'cookie cutter' Builder Grade beige carpet and white or off white walls. Ho Hum!! How is one to stand out from the next if they all followed the same advise?

Why indeed! That is NOT THE ADVISE! The advise is actually; remove distractions from your house so that the potential Buyer can "Imagine" living in each space of your house! Painting every room white is not actually 'Neutral' or necessary! Neutral is beige, dove gray, pale yellow, soft green, lavender, light blue, etc. We advise Seller's to steer clear of Dark or Bold or Florescent colors as they often dampen interest in a home if used incorrectly. Note, colors should flow not clash!

Recently, I entered a rental where the Agent/Owner watched too much DYI T.V. She had professionally had painted the dining room a rich maroon and the wall leading to the kitchen was a bluejay blue. In addition to a clashing color scheme of an open floor plan the home was laid out oddly. The hardwood floor in the kitchen didn't match the wood grain in the dining area and the transition from one to the other was not smoothly laid. The dining room had three sides, the forth should have flowed into the kitchen area not clashed with it. The bump out was separated from the kitchen by a counter and chairs. She used the bump-out for the kitchen table, this part of the room was pale yellow with tiled flooring.

The Owner was not able to be non-partial. She couldn't understand why the home just sat on the market when it had a bump-out making it one of the bigger homes in the subdivision.
As a Professional I often have to use tack to help out my client. This lady was not my client but was seeking my advice. My client and friend looked at me knowingly and smiled. He

*was a repeat client I have been friends with for at least a decade. He
and I both had a headache from sensory overload by walking through
this cacophony of color!*

*As she was an agent seeking advise I relented with providing advice
to her. She bucked at the idea of repainting, at least the dining room in
a more neutral color. She reiterated she
had just spent a lot of money to have it painted! I reminded her it had
been on the market for three months in an area most homes go under
contract within 3 weeks! We suggested she have the dining room re-
painted a beige or the same blue as the kitchen and see if it didn't help
sell the home. A lighter color would diminish the variety of flooring and
lack of flow to the home.*

*Clearly she needed to sell the house. She confided that her true
passion was not in real estate, but in dance and that she was a ballet
instructor for two different studios in Northern Virginia. She wanted to
sell the home that she had used as a rental for some years because it
was at a point where she would have to invest in maintenance in
another year or so. She took our advice and painted the dining room a
neutral color and sold the house within days for Full Price!*

Why am I expanding on the importance of paint? Painting the interior
of a home provides a sense of Newness, Cleanliness to your house. It
forces you to clean out rooms or move things around in order to do the
job correctly. Thereby, getting you into the packing up stage you will
need to do any way.

Using neutral colors gives a room a sense of spaciousness they may
not have with a darker color. By using the same color in visibly
adjacent rooms, your house will have a seamless look and a feeling of
flowing. If you desire to break up an open floor plan into 'rooms' using
color be sure to use complimentary neutral colors rather than
contrasting bold colors.

ITEM TO REMEMBER: Be sure to use window coverings that
compliment your wall color choices. Well chosen curtains, drapes or
valances are often added to a contract by the buyers because they
absolutely Love the Look the window coverings provide!

Less is More when it comes to furniture

There is value in using a Professional Stager or Interior Designer when Selling a Home. Staging is an art... the art of creating a visibly inviting living space. Consider how much money is poured into creating sets for plays as well as television shows and movie sets. In order for the audience to believe what is happening on a stage they must be transformed to the place and time depicted. Consider this when contemplating "Staging" your house.

I realize, you are not leaving your furniture behind when you move. You plan to take it with you. In the meantime let us 'use' your personal taste and style to bring about. The best
features of your house to showcase your home to every potential buyer that comes through the doors.

Creating space is different than depersonalizing a house, as such, depersonalizing will be saved for a later chapter. Creating "space" is about keeping furniture to a minimum. A prime example I often see: If a dining room is small can you live without the curio cupboard and buffet while marketing your home? It is not appealing to a Buyer to have barely enough room to walk around the dining room table because of the non-essential extra furniture in the room. All the light and neutral colors are overshadowed by a sense of being 'boxed-in.'

Yes, I understand the buffet and curio cabinet are matching pieces to the table and chairs, but you're not selling the furniture. This is not a museum. You are selling a house to people that will desire to fill it with their own items and personality. So, please remove all unnecessary furniture. If you keep fine china in the buffet and every day dishes in the kitchen cabinet realize, you can live without the china being displayed or stored in the dining room while marketing the house. Move the buffet and curio cabinet to storage ready to unpack at your destination. Do you have a study or spare empty room where you could use these pieces to showcase the room as an office or some thing else? If so, relocate the pieces to those rooms. As long as the dining room has a sense of space and freedom of moment it will flow with a potential buyer.

According to the National Association of Realtors:

Todays buyers look for Space and Storage. Even with smaller homes they look for extra storage areas.

My Step-son and I attended a Grand Opening of a New Senior Living Community in our area. The amenities were impressive... one of which was the amount of 'Storage Units' available on each floor at an additional monthly cost to the tenants. No surprise the storage units were a Big Selling Feature, and were gone before all the units were rented.

Frequently, I open a garage door or a walkout basement to see them being used as a packing area, or storage area for the move. This is OK with most buyers.   For this reason, walk through your house, or have your Agent walk through the house to be certain you have removed all obstacles from the walk ways as well as from where ones eyes fall when they enter a given room. Take the time to clear away all the clutter and dirt from closets, pantries and the laundry room. Not only clear out clutter but take time to organize them into a semblance of neatness.

I was showing rentals a few years ago and there was one in particular that my client refused to enter. Upon opening the door there were toys and clothes and an odd assortment of stuff strewn all over the front room! One look and the client said, 'forget it!' He knew it was a rental.
That didn't matter to him. What mattered is the present occupants had a lack of care for themselves as was reflected in the condition of the front room. So, he didn't care to enter into such a setting.
You are not selling your living style, you are selling a house. Focus on bring order to your home that will highlight the features of the home.

Check that high shelf in the closet and the floor of closets, pantries and laundry rooms for debris. Do they need a new coat of paint? Remember: The Little Touches often go a long way. By packing up the clutter, or weeding it out before you place your house on the market you begin the first steps of depersonalizing and get into the mode of 'letting go.' All the while you are creating flow and a sense of space that will attract a buyer to purchase your home.

Furniture placement is an easy way to highlight unique features of a house. It may also deter a buyer. I have been in homes with big living rooms that appear small because the furniture overwhelms the room. When selling, less maybe more. If you have mismatched furniture try grouping. Group a few chairs in front of a fireplace to draw attention to the hearthside warmth even on a hot summer day. If the sectional takes up all the space and is pushed tightly against the wall consider taking out all or part of the sectional and opting for something else to fill the room that can be pulled away from the wall such as a few recliners with an end table between them. Do not use an empty room for your storage area.

You want to transform that empty space into a usable, desirable space such as a guest bedroom or office, or private gym. You may even pull out some of the furniture from the living room to set up a study in the spare room. That is why renting an off site storage locker or a P.O.D. is the desired idea for the items you are planning to take with you. Keep in mind you want every room of the main home to have a purpose and be user friendly. You are creating an impression for every potential buyer. You are looking for one to say they can see themselves living there and making the whole house their own.

We are Emotion Driven

Do not be fooled into believing buyers are rational when purchasing a home. They may 'know' a home is an investment, but they buy on 'emotion' and 'feeling.' For this reason it's important to create an atmosphere of desirability. This is where that decorative touch comes in hand. A slice of greenery, and flowers on the mantel. A lit candle on the kitchen island center or in the center of the dining room table adds life to your house.   Wall art, tastefully placed in rooms or to accentuate a hall or nook. Adding a night table with a small lamp and a vase of cut flowers may spruce up a single bed with a plain blanket in a room that is otherwise bare will brighten up a small room.

Add a splash of color with a matching bedspread and curtains and perhaps a matching throw on a rocking chair or cushioned chair in a larger room. Perhaps add a few small matching pillows, or art work that carries the color or theme. When staging a room look for elements of the same color, shape, or texture to unify a room. Splashes of color should be contained to wall art or places you want to draw attention.

Note: Please remember you're selling the HOUSE not the ART! I showed a condo in Reston a few years ago. It was a small 900 square foot condo with two bedrooms and a bath. Behind the white sofa was a huge portrait that took up most of the wall! It made the room look smaller than it already was!

A big part of staging is learning the art of Balance. Balance between staging and living is big if you plan to remain until the home is sold. Seasonal decorating is possible without taking away the overall appeal of the house, but your seasonal decorating may need to be scaled back. It's important to maintain a clean, neat home free of overall distracting "Stuff."

How do you properly stage?
1. Do it yourself with a book or the internet. The downfall is the simple fact that you are emotionally invested and unable to look at your home with the detachment of a professional. Some people are very good at staging, others believe they are and would benefit from a professional. As a Realtor I do not wish to often so I may not clearly express my true opinion.

2. Hire a Professional home stager or designer. As a Realtor I have a list of professionals available for you to chose from. Just give me a call. I am here to help you reach your goal in selling your home.   I am happy to recommend other professionals to help you as well.

Keep in mind; a Great Realtor knows where to go for answers and where to find reliable resources. A new agent once asked me, 'How do you get a guy for that?'

I asked her what she met. She said all the agents that she shadowed on listing appointments would always say, 'I have a guy for that.' When asked about repairs, landscaping, staging, etc. Yes, as professionals we come in contact daily with other professionals. We may get referrals from other Professionals we work with or we may meet mortgage lenders, banker, contractors, cleaning people, etc on our own. We give them a try, if they do not work out we move on to try another until we have a list of reliable resources we feel confident in referring to others.

You only get one chance at a good First Impression! Take the time and effort and a bit of funds to give your property the very best Good Impression in order to get the best possible price for you house! It will pay-off over and over again. You will have a sense of pride with your investment and an overall knowing the job has been Well done!

6
What is ROI?

Yes, you may have Return on Investment even on your Primary property. That would be the home you live in on a regular bases. If the home was not given to you, you have a financial investment in the home. If the home was given to you, you have an emotional investment in the home.

Realize not all 'Up keep' will bring you a financial reward, but some may help you sell your home quicker. If you have a leaky roof a new roof will not necessarily improve the purchase price to equate the cost of replacement, it will however, be more appealing to a prospective buyer and therefore help you sell your home faster. The HVAC System being replaced is another one of those costly replacements that do not necessarily increase the value, but if it doesn't work when you go to sell it will hinder the sale.

I meet people regularly that believe they need a new kitchen or bathroom before they can list their home for sale. That may not be the case. Sometimes simply replacing the handset on the front door, or the kitchen faucet and cabinet knobs after a deep cleaning is sufficient.

I have had people tell me they need a new roof when it looks perfectly fine. When I ask why they point out a leak. I have a licensed contractor climb up and look and all they actually need is new chimney boots. Before you spend the money on home upgrades or repairs be certain they are what you need. A licensed contractor doesn't know your upgrade needs, that is not their specialty. A Realtor or Home

Stager is far more qualified in that area and good ones can save you money!

You may be surprised that the National Association of Realtors does an annual survey with home buyers. For the last few years one of the simplest upgrades that gives you a big bang for your buck is simply too .... Paint the front door! When it comes to home improvements to sell your house keep in mind "Less may be more."

What do I mean by that statement? Just because you remodel the kitchen and spend $15,000 doesn't mean you will increase the value of your home by $15,000.00. A new kitchen will help a house sell quickly, if done correctly, but it may not increase the over all value. So, why not spend $1,000 instead to insulate the attic to make your house more energy efficient? This may net you the same price point without spending $15,000 on an upgraded kitchen. Why? Because your return on the investment of a remodeled kitchen
equates to approximately 50% of your investment. Smaller upgrades, like replacing dated fixtures throughout the house and painting the trim will go a lot farther for a lot less.

Remodeling a perfectly good bathroom is about as useful as installing an in-ground pool to help you sell a house. The return on investment is not there. You're better off to spend your money on smaller things that make the house "Pop!"

Focus on doing necessary repairs that a home inspector would catch. Or that would show up on a loan appraisal. Especially, if VA or FHA loans are common in your area. These appraisers are trained to look for more than the average conventional appraisal is required to note. PLEASE NOTE: Most States offer Home Buying Programs based on urban or rural areas that also have income limits. These Programs often have extra work for the Appraiser or a Home Inspector to Note on a separate form. Realize these requirements by the lender of this program can make or break the deal. So, take the time and use the expert knowledge of an experienced knowledgeable handy man or service provider to make necessary repairs.

This is where a Realtor's pre-listing appointment would be helpful to you. Experienced Realtors know what a home inspector or appraiser may be looking for.

> **Often, a home seller will ask me in for a pre-listing appointment. When I walk through the home and point out things that need repaired, they will say, 'We'll do that when we get a buyer.'**
> **If you're going to wait for a buyer agree to reduce the list price to adjust for necessary home repairs or improvements.**
> **Do not expect to receive full price on a home in need of repair. Today's buyer is looking for a 'move-in-ready' home.**

Buyers should understand the Basics before buying

You may expect every home listed to meet the basic expectations. What are they? A solid roof would have been a reasonable expectation until we had the fall in 2008 - 2010 that may have been so. I took a couple to see a lovely split foyer in a nice neighborhood in Stafford in 2009. The photos on line were very promising. What didn't the photos capture? We entered a wide foyer and went upstairs and rounded the half wall to see a huge hole in the ceiling where a tree had fallen through!

It seemed the Seller's had not deemed it necessary to repair the roof or ceiling after trying to take down a tree on their own. —- It truly pays to hire a professional in many areas. A professional tree removal company has insurance to cover such accidents should they occur. They also have the hands on training to know how to cut the tree to avoid such costly accidents.

Needless to say, my buyers were looking for a 'good deal.' Not a big repair job. Like many home buyers they wanted a move-in ready home at a 'fixer up' price. They actually admitted they would have considered getting a rehab loan on this home if it had not been located right next to the community drain pipe and a large gully. With small children and no fence near the gully they decided the cost of both the roof, ceiling and needing a fence would not be in their budget. Additionally, the wife was concerned with the possibility of mold as the hole had been in the roof long enough to have seedlings and moss growing around it and it was the rainy spring season.

Water damage is always a concern with buyers as there is the potential for mold. If you've had a water leak be sure to complete the repairs as well as the restoration work. When you replace a roof boot or the roof entirely and leave water stains on the ceiling you have essentially negated the value of your efforts. Be sure to repaint the ceilings of the effected closets as well as the whole room. A messy paint job where you have paint streaks, or brush marks over lines is not any better than leaving the water stain. A professional paint job is well worth the money!

Be sure your gutters and down spouts are cleaned and properly attached. Check the foundation for cracks. Have the Heating and Air Conditioning Unit inspected and cleaned. Is your sub-flooring solid? Level? When I walk across a floor and its uneven… that's a problem I will highlight to the potential buyer and ask the Home Inspector if an Engineer is needed.

> I listed a Bank owned home in Fredericksburg with a cracked foundation. After having two potential buyers walk away on the home inspection the Bank agreed to have an engineer come out. This was money well spent. The Engineer's team was able to repair it for $6,000 and the home sold for full asking price, $353,000.00

Realizing what's important is the key to selling your house quickly. Understand the market value of your house is determined by the prices of those homes that have recently sold within your subdivision, or area. In a city that may be just a few blocks. In a rural setting the appraiser may need to expand several miles or look for comparable beyond three months old. This is why, remodeling your kitchen or master bath may be a 'Wow' factor but it may not bring you more money than your neighbors house. It's important to realize some improvements will cost you more money than you will get in return.

Maintenance that Must be done!

It's easy for both the Seller and Buyer to get caught up on what is attractive to the eye when making a major purchase such as a home. That's why the Home Inspector and Appraiser plays such and important role in the process. They are objective eyes coming from two different perspectives.

All to often Landlords and Homeowners over look the importance of regular maintenance on the unseen systems of a house. These often come to light during the selling process. *For that there are an abundance of Home Warrantee Companies selling policies for what may happen in that first year of transition. When you are ready to sell your home be sure to ask the Listing Agent about placing a Home Warrantee on your home. For a nominal service fee this warrantee will cover major repairs like appliances that fail in the first 12 months of a home sale. When it comes to the HVAC most companies will initially tell you they cover the Heating and Air Condition, but if you actually need a replacement you will be lucky to get 50% of the cost from the warrantee company.*

Take a moment to check a few of your mechanical features:

- ✦ *Is the Electrical box and wiring up to code?*
- ✦ *Have the Heating and Cooling system cleaned and checked.*
- ✦ *Check the natural gas lines for leaks*
- ✦ *Is the plumbing in good working order?*
- ✦ *If on well & septic you will be required to pump the septic prior to closing.*
- ✦ *You want to have your septic company do a walk over to check for leaks*
- ✦ *Have you well water tested for potability*
- ✦ *Check the roof for leaks, especially around vents and boots*
- ✦ *Check the basement or crawl space for leaks and mold.*

Keep in mind these components wear out. If they are not in good working order you should lower the sales price of your home to compensate for the disrepair.

A home inspector will be looking at these items. I have had a number of Condos and Townhomes in the Reston area of Virginia in need of replacing the Electrical Box based on the home inspection. There was a certain brand that was known to have electrical fire issues. Keep in mind that once a Home Inspector notices one thing in a home they often find additional items of note. Different Inspectors may have different knowledge and experience. I had one that had knowledge with HVAC systems and sure enough there was an issue with the heating systems burners that the Home Inspector picked up on.

A Home Inspector will take the cover off the Electrical Panel to make certain the circuits are not overloaded and all wires are grounded to prevent fire issues. So, if you need a junction box now, before you list, is the time to invest on an Electrician coming out to correctly add additional boxes, breakers, outlets, etc. Removing an issue before it becomes an obvious issue is the best course of action when dealing with home safety issues.

In this day and age a Home Buyer expects to have a working central air and heating system in the homes they purchase. Opening the back door and front door with the ceiling fans going may have worked in the 1970's, but that form of cooling does not work in this day and age!

People want to purchase a home that is Safe and Sound. They look to see if there are Smoke Detectors, check for lead based paint, and mold and even radon. People with small children or planning to raise a family in the home they buy may avoid homes too close to an above ground power line. Where my sister lives in Ohio, many homeowners avoid the oil pipelines. You can sometimes smell the oil as you drive by! Can you imagine living with that smell daily?

Keep in mind that buyers are looking for a home that reflects their aesthetic tastes and lifestyles. They want something safe and comfortable that will work for them. Faulty electric systems are scary and may cost you a sale. Leaky plumbing brings 'mold issues' to mind. This can be costly to remedy depending on how long the issues has been allowed to continue and the amount of damage done. Sewage and drainage issues can also cause health issues that may cause a potential buyer to walk away.

In the long run it's better to disclose the issues up front and if necessary reduce the list price to compensate for the estimated repair or remediate or repair before putting the house on the market. One way or another you will pay for these necessary and perhaps costly repairs.

It is always in your best interest to pay for a professional to do any and all mechanical work. Be certain they are licensed or insured or work for a company that warrantees their work.

✚   If a Handyman did a plumbing repair have a Certified Plumber inspect the entire water system for leaks. (the Professional Plumber will not inspect someone else work, but they will look for leaks.)

✚   Be sure to call to have your well checked for portable water. A Buyer's Lender will usually ask for a water test as well. There are two different test... it depends on the lender.

But if you check before listing you can make any necessary remedies required before they become an issue.

✦ Have the Septic System Inspected before listing for any leaks. This will come out during the appraisal or septic inspection so it is best to check in advance.

✦ Call your HVAC Company to have your system service and inspected. Ask them to look at the Hot Water Heater and Sump Pumps while they are out there servicing the Heating and Cooling Systems. Some will tell you they do not handle those units. Others will be qualified.

✦ Ask your natural gas supplier to inspect your tanks and lines, and any appliances or fireplace they are connected too.

✦ Arrange for a chimney sweep to clean the chimney and inspect the outside of the chimney.

✦ Be sure all your windows and outside doors open and close properly. Having a window that doesn't align just right may worry a potential buyer about foundation issues. Reseal those windows that show signs of a broker seal. You want a prospective buyer to see a well maintained home.

As I mentioned before, you may save time by simply calling a qualified, or Certified Home Inspector and ask them if they are qualified to make the above inspections all in one visit. A Certified Home Inspector will be able to spot any trouble areas or potential trouble areas for you. By addressing potential issues prior to marketing the home for sale you have avoid issues that could cause a buyer to walk away. Once you have a list of necessary repairs and estimates of cost you can decided to make the repairs or adjust the selling price to accommodate the need for those repairs.

Replacing Appliances

Undoubtedly, new appliances provide a 'Wow' factor. This is a regional issue. When I lived in New York State one expected to purchase their own refrigerator and perhaps a stove when one moved to a new location. I even knew people that had to install their own kitchen cabinets when they purchased a home. But throughout Virginia it is common for the appliances to convey. When I moved to

Fredericksburg I worked with a Real Estate Broker that would tell Sellers to go to Sears and put all new appliances on their credit card to sell a house. They could pay off the card with the proceeds from the closing. Many of them simple put it on the HUD1 statements to be paid by the Title Company upon closing. It's important to know local market expectations when selling a house. You may need to adjust your expectations to get your house sold.

Why did my Fredericksburg Broker Judy insist that Home Sellers go into debt for new appliances?

The National Association of Realtors conducted a survey of Home Buyers. They found that:

- Buyers were somewhat more interested in buying a home with new features like matching kitchen appliances than homes that did not come with matching appliances.
- Even though approximately only 17% of Buyers preferred 'Stainless Steel' it became the norm for Realtors to suggest to a Seller over a ten year period.
- Most Buyers are willing to pay on average $2,000 to $5,000 more on the purchase price to get the matching stainless steel appliances.

Lesson learned: If you want top dollar for your home realize it may require you to spend money wisely up front. So, if you can afford it… do it!

If replacing all the kitchen appliances is the option you have chosen it may set your property apart from a similar one across the street. If this is not in your budget the alternative is to throughly give your fully functioning appliances a good deep cleaning.

This is a time to really look at the condition of Kitchen counters, shelves, cabinet doors and knobs. Are they warn looking? Can you afford to replace? Do you know how to clean and shine wood surfaces to make them more appealing? You need to consider these questions before you put your property on the market.

After you list is not the time to repair and update. Those first buyers and agents to see the property will talk. The National Association of Realtors can show you statistics where repairs after listing negatively impact the sales price.

Note: A few years ago I found a couple a home in King George. We got to the Home Inspection and when the Inspector turned on the gas oven a plume of flames shot out when we opened the oven door! It frightened the wife and children to the point they canceled the purchase of this seemingly lovely home.

Note regarding Hardware:

Walk through your bathrooms and kitchen. Is the hardware worn? tarnished? missing? mismatched? If you answer, 'Yes,' then it is best to replace all the hardware and give each room a thorough cleaning! Consider, when you looked at this house as a buyer; would it not be more appealing with a fresh, updated look? Cleaning and new hardware may give you that little extra.

Keep in mind if your handles, pulls, knobs and hinges are broken or mismatched it is better to replace them. It's amazing how far a bit of sprucing up with new hardware, a good cleaning, or sanding, and paint can do to transform something worn into something new.

A few years ago my husband and I purchased a home that had been vacant. The Sellers had done a deep cleaning and painted the trim a dove gray. After we moved in and I was cleaning the bathroom I realized that the tiles had been painted that dove gray rather than being dove gray tiles!

An Inspector is not looking for paint to cover up tile. They focus on hidden electrical and water issues. They may or may not use a heat sensor on walls and ceiling to see if the walls and ceilings are efficient. They check the roof, and windows to be certain the roof is sound and the windows all work. They check water pressure, and if there are any leaks.

That said please consider:
A little effort upfront goes a Long Way!

- Towel bars
- Toilet paper holders
- Door handles
- Are the light fixtures dated? Rusty?
- In the kitchen is there an attached paper towel role?
- Is the toilet seat in good shape? Consider purchasing a new one.

Other touches to consider:

- Re-grout or repair around tile on any backsplash, floors, tubs and showers.
- Consider Refurbish tired-looking or blistered cabinet doors with sanding and a fresh   coat of stain, a finish or paint.
- Can you replace a dated or stained bathroom sink? This small investment may have a huge impact on selling your house quickly.

Touching up your home without breaking the bank may go a long way into selling quickly at a great price. It pays to seek out ideas in magazines or the internet. 'Pinterest' and 'Youtube', "how to" books and videos at the public library can be a wealth of information.

Be sure all doors with deadbolts have matching hardware that properly opens and closes with ease.

Ample Light!

This includes natural light from windows, doors, skylights, as well as artificial light goes a long way to showing off your house. Pick up a copy of "LUXURY HOMES," invariably you will see a few photos of 'high-end' homes at night or at twilight with all the lights a blazing! This is showing off the houses, 'ambiance.'

Lighting plays a big part in Staging a house For Sale. The Agents advertising in the Luxury Homes Magazine understands the significance of utilizing natural lighting to transform a high end home into a show piece. Those blazing lights against the dark of night softens the homes features while making it stand out again the night skies. Keep in mind, Harsh lighting has an opposite effect. It is often unflattering. Poor lighting is not only *bad for your eyes,* it may also give a home a dingy overall feel.

Most prospective buyers look at homes during the daylight hours. Sometimes homes are shown late in the evening. For this reason consider the importance of additional lighting where needed thorough out the house. Rooms with small windows need lamps or ceiling lights to support the natural light. Increase the wattage of the light bulbs.

If you have 'energy efficient' bulbs in hall outlets that take a moment to warm up it is worthwhile to replace them prior to showing. Buyers do not want to wait for the lights to 'warm up,' before they walk through the hall or where ever the energy efficient bulbs are. This is a deterrent rather than a positive.

Be certain the lighting fixtures you have or are purchasing goes with the room. The globe lights on a chain may have been stylish in the 1970's but they are not popular today. Just as pendant lighting works well in a kitchen with high ceilings and not in any room with low ceilings.

Generally, there are four kinds of lighting. Natural lighting, this may come from high windows or skylights. *Some ethnic groups look for natural lighting to fall in the living room or kitchen in order to be enticed to buy.* I have shown many a home that lack these simple considerations. Ambient lighting is general lighting, over head lighting. Pendant lighting is wonderful over a kitchen counter for those who love cooking, or in a reading room with a high ceiling. Lastly, you have accent light these are on tables, recessed in the ceiling to highlight a feature of the home, or a personal item. They maybe wall sconces, or backlighting for an extra touch, or under the kitchen cabinets. Lighting is a wonderful way to bring out the best features of your house.

Consider key areas like the Foyer to set the stage with a great first impression to prospective buyers. This is why so many homes opt for a lovely chandelier type fixture in a foyer and perhaps also in the dining room. If the ceilings are low you may benefit from wall sconces. Wall scones add a bit of charm in smaller spaces. Keep in mind, your goal with lighting is to make certain each area or room is effective lit.

Focus on the Foyer, Kitchen and bathrooms. These rooms are pivot rooms for any prospective buyer. The kitchen and bathrooms can make or kill a sale. A well lit kitchen may feature a combination of natural lighting, ambient lighting and perhaps track lighting under the cabinets. Track lighting is a great way to make a granite counter top shine! Be sure you have ample lighting over the sink as this is a much used area of the house. Point: if you have a hood or exhaust fan over the stove be sure to have new, clear bulbs put in to ensure all is bright for your prospective buyers!

Bathroom lights should be intense without being harsh. If you need separate switches between the shower area and the sink area… invest in providing these separate areas with proper lighting. Soft white is a good approach for a bathroom.

Avoid harsh lighting in the bedroom. Lamps often have a switch for one or more outlets deemed for room lamps. This is a place for natural lighting in combination with soft, peaceful lighting. This is a room where you want to feel at peace and a place one can rest. Going with a soft green, gray, ecru or lavender in this room gives it a warm, cozy feel and prevents it from feeling drab. You want this room to be set an impression of comfort. All too often I see Home Seller's paint all the rooms white and remove every picture, photo, and paintings from the walls. This is often a mistake because the house becomes harsh and uninteresting. Despite what others say... You want Your House to leave a Positive Mental Impression! Help the prospective buyer remember your house over all the other houses they're looking at by leaving color or personality in some of the rooms!

Flooring:

Many Home Seller's and agents may over look the 1000 pound gorilla in the room, but you can be certain prospective Buyer's will notice! When you purchased the 'Cheapest' home in the subdivision a few years ago the low grade vinyl flooring may have been OK. But now, it's showing signs of wear and all your neighbors have ceramic tile. Believe me, unless you're in the trades flooring should not be a 'Do It Yourself' Project. I can not stress enough how many homes I have shown that did not sell because the flooring was 'off.' One that comes to mind was a high end home in a sought after subdivision. The Home Owner had put the hard wood floor in the kitchen at an angle... it seemed to have been to separate it from the living room in an Open Floor Plan. It hurt the eyes to look at it and it was the first thing the Buyers commented on!

Keep in mind, floors in bad shape will devalue your home in the eyes of any buyer very quickly! This includes the stairs. On the other hand... If you have installed new carpet on the stairs and beautiful hardwoods recently, you will have buyers willing to pay top dollar for that clean, fresh look!

Scrimping on shabby carpets by thinking a good cleaning will be OK will not cut it with buyers or renters. It is not a wise investment to invest in cabinet 'refacing' and gutter guards if you have stained carpet or poorly installed hardwood floors. If money is tight see if a professional will 'cut in' a matching piece of carpet, or if your floors can withstand a stripe and sanding. Add a Thorough cleaning and you may come out just as well.

I've known a number of 'Flipper's' that imagined getting rich by buying low and selling high only to find out that didn't work because flooring is not always as easy as you may think. If you're not certain what you should do - Take Stock.

Make notes for yourself from the prospective of a home buyer. Move the furniture... it will not be there when you leave. Are there stains? Blemishes? Fading?

Make a list: what should be replaced. What could be cleaned? What could be repaired? Would the carpets be OK with a good steaming? Do you need to rent an 'Odor Eliminating' machine? Should you replace the carpet in pathways with a different type of flooring?

Take the time to look at homes similar to yours that are presently "For Sale." Go to "Estate Sales" in your area, as well as a few "Open Houses." If you own a double wide or modular, take the time to go to a House Lot and look at the homes there. Mentally, compare your home flooring and fixtures to what they have. Does your's compare? Is it nicer than what you see? Or do you need to do some work? Could you manage with a really deep cleaning or do you need to make some replacements? This includes color by the way. Some colors date a house, Like the popular 'salmon pink' plush carpet of the 1980's. Or a really dark Green carpet. If the color dates the carpet it also dates the house. Keep in mind the age of the majority of home buyers in your area. They are looking for something 'new,' 'fresh.' Carpet generally last seven to ten years so if your carpets color dates it beyond that time frame it should be replaced.

Real wood flooring adds quality to a home that laminate simply can not meet. True hardwood can be refinished by a flooring professional to rejuvenate the appearance. In todays market people often went for thinner flooring or composite.. this type of hardwood may or may not be refinished. Just as Tile laid properly should stand up well. However, if it was not there maybe cracks and it may be difficult to match the tile.

Would you be happy with a kitchen floor that has two different tiles?

Maybe your eyes are not as good as they once were. You may think the two color are close enough... I can assure you... buyers and agents will notice! It will negatively impact the sales price! Don't do it!

Chances are a prospective buyer will not be impressed with mismatched tiles any where in the house. One thing I can tell you from years of experience... penny wise today is pound foolish tomorrow when it comes to home upgrades and repairs. You truly get what you pay for in the long run. I have so often heard of people going with the cheapest guy and he started the job and never finished. Or he did such a bad job they had to hirer someone else to come fix the first guys work... no savings there!

As My Husband is an HVAC (Heating, Ventilation and Air Conditioning) Professional I must insert a pet peeve here…. PLEASE, PLEASE, PLEASE do not scrimp on an HVAC System!! It is TRULY IMPORTANT to have your whole house HVAC system cleaned annually if you desire to have the system last a long time! If you have Pets you should change your filters monthly. If you have no pets or children you should change or clean the filters bi-montly.

If you believe your system needs replaced there are some key points to NOTE:
A.   Be sure the indoor unit matches the outdoor unit. Mismatched units effect the efficiency of both units as well as may effect your energy bill.
B.   If you are told you need a new unit please get a second opinion before investing $3,000 to $30,000 for a system replacement.
C. Be sure you are replacing your unit with a comparable unit both in size and efficiency.

It is remarkable how many Seller's believe a Buyer or their Home Inspector will not notice an undersized unit has just been installed. Advertising 'New' HVAC and not have it properly sized is not a selling point. Especially, if a potential buyer walks through on a particularly cold or hot day and notices one floor is substantially different in temperature than the other floor.

Thinking about Kitchens & Baths

Recently, I went on a listing appointment where they had made the half bath as you enter the house into a full bath by extending the wall to add a walk-in shower. Great! Until I went to the laundry room. They moved the wall making the laundry room not only tiny but they did not move the window that faced the Front of the House! Yep... the wall essentially cut the window in half and the half to the bathroom was closed off, but still visible from the front porch! Ugh! Does that sound appealing? Would you pay $450,000 for that house on an acre of land in a subdivision? BE WISE WITH UPGRADES! BE SURE THEY MAKE SENSE AND FLOW WITH THE HOUSE!

I do not want to be the one to tell you that your $10,000 new bathroom devalued the home because you didn't place it the right way. Someone should have told this couple the Key to renovations and upgrades is to consider 'Mass Appeal' when it comes to 'Resale' Value.

Last summer I went Townhome Shopping with a friend and her daughter. We went into a 'Flip' townhome, at first glance the kitchen was bright and clean. We looked around and quickly noticed the backsplash tiles pattern was upside down. The snap together wood flooring had gaps that would get bigger once the floor settled. Additionally, this was the highest priced townhome in the neighborhood. The 'Flipper' was hosting the "Open House" and was obviously pleased with the kitchen and didn't seem to notice it was not done correctly. Even though I said nothing my girlfriend and her daughter both noticed everything and was not interested in that home at any price!

You need not go into debt to sell your home! Sometimes a kitchen is fine with a great cleaning and new appliances. Or simply refinished flooring. When it comes to kitchens, you want to go for mass appeal. What's presently in 'Style,' or what is on the cutting edge of style. You want fresh and appealing as the kitchen is a Predominate place in any home. Let's get there while still having a Return on Investment.

Go for neutral colors that help the flow of the home. In Massachusetts I walked into a kitchen with white birch painted on a black wall on one wall the length of the room! The opposite wall was a galley styled kitchen with blue gray coloring below white cabinets. It left an indelible impression in my mind, but I am not certain I would say it was a positive impression. Again, the homeowner very proudly announced she had painted the wall herself. Who am I to tell her this will not help to sell the home? I am a Professional that sees hundreds of homes and buyers annually. If you plan to paint a unique mural on one wall please make certain it does not clash with the rest of the room!

On the flip side, I went into a home with a beautiful garden mural painted at the top of the stairs. There was a hand painted white stone frame on a neutral wall that correlated to the painting. That home had multiple offers and was very well received.

Consider: Neutral colors that accent the homes structure and style.
  * Have a stylish backsplash added to the kitchen for a clean, fresh look

  * Consider adding new counter tops if your cabinets are in good shape.

  * A new Modern Kitchen Faucet may be all you need.

  * If you can add a pantry, or cabinet space consider this option. I had a home in Fredericksburg that had narrow pantry shelves. I added wider shelving and a broom closet at the end of the hall... it changed the whole look for very little effort!

  * Small half baths look bigger with a pedestal sink, but a woman likes a vanity.

  * Consider new toilet seats with matching paper holders.

Are Buyers in your area concerned with Utility Bills?

If they're asking for average utilities or copies of your most recent bills they are concerned. What can you do about it?

  ^ Consider Installing an updated 'energy-saving' smart thermostat that saves on utility bills and can be monitored from your phone. (Be aware, that if you have an older system a newer thermostat may not work with it.)

^ Install solar vents in the attic space that helps expel hot air in the summer. *This made a big difference on a house I purchased a few years ago. After moving out I rented it and the renters were pleased with the low electric bills. I purchased the solar fan at Costco for about $239.00, paid a local contractor another $200.00 to install it and it has added value ever since!*

Make Space!!

The National Association of Realtors survey buyers every year. Buyer always note Closet Space after closing on a house. People love Walk-in Closets. Small closets were fine in the 1800's when people only had two or three outfits. They do not work for the majority of people today. When I looked at the 'Tiny House' models all I could think of was the fact we would need a second one for storage of our clothes and 'stuff' we want to keep! When people accumulate a bunch of possessions they need the space to store it. George Carlson said it best, 'we start out content in an apartment and out grow it with all our stuff!'

* Buyers want a laundry room. Preferably, on the same level as the bedrooms. But DO NOT spend money on Creating a space where there is no room!

* Buyers want a bathroom linen closets, perhaps you have vacant space at the end of the hall that will work. It's important to hire someone that knows how to make changes look like they belong there.

* Garages with storage sell faster than ones without. Be sure you can still park a car and be able to open the doors after the storage is added. Otherwise, it's not worth adding.

* Buyers look for a walk-in kitchen pantry. It's not absolutely necessary. It often depends on the price point of the home.

Bottom line... great storage space sells homes throughout the country! That being said, I would not expand a master bath at the expense of a walk-in closet. When modernizing an

older home finding larger closet space will certainly help the resale value as much as finding space for a second bathroom in a one bathroom home.   Perhaps converting an old out dated
3 bedroom home into a 2 bedroom, 2 bath home will make it more appealing and sell faster. If space is limited and rooms are small another option is a closet organizer that maximizes the closet space you have.

Consider creating storage space in an attic or basement area that would be appealing to a prospective buyer.

Now, that you're in the organizing mode… keep going! This is a great time to organize your cabinets. Look at your laundry room and linen closet… less is more when it comes to personal items. Remember, I mentioned adding shelf space in the pantry? Extra Shelving may be as simple as adding width to existing shelves or adding Extra shelves in the laundry and linen closet is a big help too. People like space for folding and hanging laundry in a Laundry room. A sense of space and room for their storage in these places can make a big impact.

Consider the dead space at the end of a hall. We hired a handy man to come turn that space into a linen closet in a split foyer we had purchased. It was well received by buyers that came to an Open House.

** **Make sure any improvements to add space and storage are tasteful. You may enjoy the benefits of increased storage as well.**

**Consider the effort of Statics when Selling your home.
Published Features Home Buyers seek:**

+ Energy Star-rated appliances

+ Laundry room on the same floor as the bedrooms

+ Exhaust fan in the bathroom

+ Allowance of natural lighting

+ Bathroom linen closet

+ Energy Star-rated windows

+ Ceiling Fans - In your area do people prefer with lights attached or without lights?

+ Garage Storage

+ Space for eat-in kitchen or combo kitchen

** The above mentioned features may not necessarily be effective or profitable. However, if they are tastefully done they add value and help sell the home.

Also consider negative features that deter Buyers:

■   Master bath with only a small shower stall

■   Small closet spaces

■   Only 1 bathroom

■   Narrow two-story family room

■   Wet bar

■   Laminate or chipped countertops

■   Built-in Glass Front Cabinets

The most successful home sellers take time before listing to declutter, depersonalize and invest in deep cleaning and staging their home.

Please note: Functional Obsolescence is a negative you may or may not be able to over come. If the home is in a sought after location it is not as important as if the home is in an average location.

In 2004 I was working on a development project with a long time friend. She insisted that the condos and townhomes should have at least two bathrooms if not more. At the time, I thought she was a little excessive about that point as it made the bedrooms smaller. Fast forward just five years and it turned out she was right!

We had both grown up in large families with one bathroom and shared bedrooms. She had moved to a tourist area where I remained in a rural area to sell real estate. From her experience with tourist rentals she saw the change in the market regarding multiple bathrooms before it became a given.

In no time at all the one bathroom home became obsolete across America!

Flash forward to 2016: In order to make a small condo more salable in Northern Virginia I have seen creative Sellers add a half bath where you would expect to find a closet in the master bedroom. They hadn't even changed out the sliding mirrored door where the closet had been.

Additionally, I have seen people add a stackable in their outdoor storage shed of a townhouse to add a half bath off-the-kitchen where the side by side washer and drier had been. These changes may seem unusual, but in truth they helped sell the home. They left a positive, memorable impression.

Realize that those who take the time to make obvious repairs and adjustments as well as a deep cleaning and declutter prior to listing sell their home sell that home 10 times faster than those that wait until the first pass of buyers goes through.

You only get one chance to make a great first impression! Make it your best!

Where to Begin?

Begin Mentally & Physically with Depersonalize

You may think, Mentally has no relevance when it comes to a Seller. You would be WRONG! Mentally, you must 'Let Go,' before you can truly be willing to Sell your home!

It's not the same as an investment property. You are not emotionally attached to an investment property. You are attached emotionally to where you live. This emotion may be positive or negative... it is reflected in every aspect of the home and believe me when I say, Buyers sense it!.

If you have signs all over your house that says, "Do not touch." Or you want to sell by "Appointment Only," these a HUGE RED FLAGS you are not ready to sell. Buyers sense it and generally will skip even a physical peek if there is another similar home that is ready.

Think back to when I mentioned Staging. Remember? When you're ready to sell your home it's important to begin the step of mentally letting go. You want the prospective buyer to be able to visualize living in this house - without you. Without your personal touch. It's OK to leave a few personal things to show the home, but start packing up trophies, the wall of family photos and collectibles as a way to physically let go. When you go off to work while your house is on the market, put away you dirty laundry, your dirty dishes, last nights bowl of uneaten popcorn. Be presentable within a 30 minute window for a showing at any time! That is not easy for everyone. But if you can adjust your life style for a few weeks or months it takes to sell your house you will be well on your way to moving out by closing time.

It's time to let someone else make it their home.

It's OK to have one or two family photos on the wall or a special award or meaningful painting that wows the room. But these items will not be left for new owners, so why not pack them up? Knickknacks collect dust and are often deemed personalized to someones taste, so if you have a curio cupboard filled it's time to begin packing. If they are very meaningful try to pack away as many as you can and leave just a few spaced sporadically on the shelves. Remember: Less is more. If you have distracting wall decor you may wish to pack that up as well.

NOTE: Pole dancing may keep you firm, but having it in your master bedroom when I show prospective buyers is not a turn-on or a selling tool. Taking it down will bring a better value to your home. These types of personal items are best packed up prior to photographing the house for Listing.

Storage units can be rented and delivered on site or off site and its worth the monthly fee.

Why do I move every Five to Ten years?

American's are a society of collectors and good intensions. I am no different from anyone else... I collect children's artwork, cute outfits, postcards, trinkets from trips and vacations over the years. But I choose to move every few years to force myself not to collect a life time of STUFF!

A few years ago a neighbor decided to retire to another country. They had lived in their home for thirty years. Raised their two children there and had traveled extensively for work and for pleasure. Needless to say they had a lot of Trinkets with sentimental value as well as monetary value. But they could not take it all with them. What to keep and what to let go?

My thought is if we move every three to seven years, even if its just around the corner I will continually expunge all the frivolous stuff we enjoyed for a time but now it's time to share with others while it still has value and meaning.

Yes, I left my forty two year old husband's college books and magazines that were twenty years old in the attic of the first home we purchased together. I left my daughter's Pink and White Barbie doll house she had out grown in the attic of another home when she was thirteen. Sometimes its best to 'leave a gift' for someone else than let a loved one remember they forgot something they no longer needed anyway.

Moving forces you to DECLUTTER and DISCARD!!

When the mover comes and quotes you a price it's base on pounds. The less you have to move the cheaper it will be and the easier it will be. I know you like having your large bowl of
endless popcorn next to your recliner and all the mail from the year piled on the top of the frog, but now is the time to sort the mail and throw out all the ads you do not need! Now, is the time to limit that popcorn to sitting next to you only a few hours a night when no one will be calling to take a tour.

Now, is the time your grown daughter needs to come get her bedroom set you have shoved to the side of an over crowded room. If she doesn't it's time to post it for new owners to come and claim. You worked out presenting Curb Appeal on the outside of your home. Now, is the time to create curb appeal inside the home.

Thin out the books, magazines, DVD Collections, crafts that have dust because you haven't had time to finish them. Either pack them up or give them away as they are. The more spacious your home appears the more appealing it will be for a prospective buyer. This is the time to Minimize without compromise. You still wish to enjoy 'living' in the comfort of your home until it's sold. But you can do this without keeping all the stuff you're not presently using or working on. You want the prospective Buyer to be able to imagine your home has all they are looking for. They are not your guest. You need not be 'Show room' perfect, but stand back and see where you can live without all the clutter and comfort that makes it your own. This is the time to paint over the finger prints 'Johnny left ' on the ceiling when he was five years old. Take a photo and then 'away they go!'

As you pack up you will feel the release. Letting go slowly often makes moving much easier. Take a moment to jot down some of the memories that flow through you as you pack up. This is another way to free your spirit of the ties that anchored you to this home. Once written you can share those memories later in your new home with loved ones and those that made those experiences so happy and enjoyable for you. Don't spend to much time in writing… just let them flow and then get back to packing!!

Imagine, you're new home is waiting for you to let this one go! It's clean and fresh, and ready for you to move in! That's just what you need to do to this one as you pack up and go!

Are you a Planner? A List Maker?

I am a list maker when we're going on vacation. I have had to become a list maker as a parent for children that struggle to remember chores. But over all it did not come naturally.

Moving works best when you make a Plan

I have worked through the fall out of 2005 - 2008. You know you're going to list a short sale when you walk into a home of chaos. Prospective Buyers know it too. In addition to the home generally being in a state of havoc, and in need of repair the prospective buyer had to be willing to wait usually over a year for the bank to accept their offer. By the time they moved in the place was worst than when they initially saw it.

That is not how home transfers should go! You want your home to radiate warmth, charm. A pleasant place to be, happy memories, what ever that may be.

Keep in mind… people are driven by their emotions! The sense of Smell makes an amazing and under valued subconscious stir of emotions. Please be sure your home smells refreshing and comforting!

A list or a plan is a good place to begin!

- List each room —- make a note of the clutter, including closets and built in shelves
Do you have pets that have left scratches or marks any where?

- Take a deep breath. Or get some help to begin decluttering. Have a clothes basket for what doesn't go and boxes for what you plan to take. Start with the smaller space first. It's easier to tackle small spaces and you feel you've accomplished something when you stop for a break. By using the clothes basket and emptying it into large trash bags or boxes to donate you'll also feel yourself letting go and getting into the desire to move. Moving is not only a physical process… it's a mental process.

- Only leave essential items in each room, unless you're an interior designer and have a knack for leaving a few light touches. Again, less is more. You're staging your home for the potential buyer to envision themselves living there. Some people are so talented that buyers have requested buying some of the furniture in the home… because it went so well in the room!

- Now, you have your piles to be donated or discarded its easy to keep going! You're on a roll where you'll want to pack up as little as possible to take to your next home. Donating can be fun! Throwing away broken toys no one ever repaired and old newspaper clippings lifts ones spirit. You go outside and enjoy the sunshine!

- You pack up those possessions you want to see in your new home, but can live without in the current home. They're ready for storage. We all know someone that moved two years ago and they can't park in their garage because it's still filled with storage boxes from the move.   I would suggest those packed boxes should be donated as well. We have some in our garage. Mostly, ours are business paperwork we're required to keep for seven years by the IRS. I enjoy scrapping a few every year when they hit the mark to be burned or shedded!

■   OK, You think you've decluttered all you can. Look around. Are surfaces clean and free of collected things? Can you see your kitchen table? How about the island? Be sure surfaces are clean and clear each time your home is scheduled to be shown. Remember: showings work best when you are not there!

As I said... I'm not generally a List Person
I became one out of necessity. So for those of you that are. Here you go....

Go through your house Room by Room!

— **Kitchen:** This is a pivotal room and should always be spotlessly tidy yet inviting. Clear the counters. If you have long or wide counters you can leave 3 or 4 essential items. Put away towels, dishrags, and potholders. It's tempting to leave a dish towel with a cute saying like "This Home is filled with KISSES, wagging tails & wet noses" on the towel rack... make sure its clean without stains though.

Be sure to clear out under the sink so you have room to store soaps and cleaners. Pack away rarely used small appliances and serving dishes. Anything you only use for special occasions should be packed away now. If you have decorative built-in shelving you wish to showcase you can leave out a few teacups and platters. Pack up any seasonal dishes and accessories you have. Remove pest control traps or poison from the pantry and closets. Appliances should not be used for storage. Buyers do not want to find bread in the microwave or dirty pans in the oven.

Be sure the pantry is clean and organized. You want them to envision how wonderfully roomy a pantry can be (regardless of the size of your pantry!)

— **Dining Areas:** Some homes no longer have a formal dining room. The open concept homes simply have a space near the kitchen. Clear off any flat surfaces… especially the table. (I have been in homes where the table is set as if for a dinner party with table cloth, center piece and a matching set out on display. This is OK, please do not leave out the silverware!

Subtle decor like a vase of flowers or a basket of fruit is a nice touch.

— **Living room/ Family area:** I often go to others homes and see all the books, DVD's, Magazines, throws, remotes, and what nots sprinkled here and there. It's the 'Common Area.' This is the time to clean up! Clear flat surfaces. Decorate a container for your remotes, and magazines and electronics. Put away the ones you don't need. Clear up built in bookcases so there is a lot of 'open space' on the shelves. Fold and drape throws neatly over the back of the sofa or chair.

— **Bathrooms:** Remove all your stuff from the counters! PLEASE: take the time to close the toilet lid when you leave the room. Empty the cabinets and drawers. Keep what you need in the cabinets and drawers and either pack up the rest or through it away. BE CERTAIN TO STORE PRESCRIPTION MEDICINE OUT OF SIGHT AND REACH OF CHILDREN! I can not stress this enough.

In 2018 it was reported a Realtor in Richmond lost his real estate license because he
showed a home that had prescription medication on top of the refrigerator.
He went back on his own and took some of the medicine, not realizing the
home had cameras throughout for security.

Keep in mind Real Estate Agents, Consultants, Brokers, are people. They may not alway keep a close eye on their clients and their clients children at all times. Please Avoid issues by taking precaution.

Find a safe place for jewelry, keepsakes, and perfumes. Store hair products and styling tools on closet shelves or in cabinets. Make the bathroom look like its rarely used.

This may be an inconvenience for many, but it will be well worth the extra effort in the long run.

— **Bedrooms:** By now it may sound repetitive. But Neatness counts! Be in the habit of Making your Bed every morning! Especially, when your house is on the market! Sometimes you only have an hours notice! Put away valuables and small things. Keep your rooms as tidy as possible. Be sure a prospective Buyer can walk thru each room. Buyers understand you're living in the home, but they also want to see you appreciate what you have.

— **Linen Closets:** PLEASE take a moment to Organize and clean out! Pack up seasonal blankets, sheets, seasonal outer wear, etc. Store everything you're not using away to storage. Keep linens to a minimum… like one change for each bed size or each room.

— **Laundry Room:** Many of the bigger homes in our market have more than one laundry room. This works great for larger families! Our house has one on the first floor we use and one on the second floor the children use. Whether your washer & drier are stackable in the basement, a laundry room, or a laundry closet you should make the room and area neat.

Perhaps you need to purchase a space saver to tuck away the detergent and drier sheets between the washer and drier or in the small space next to the washer and drier. Neat and Orderly sells homes! Do you have a cabinet or shelf for deterent, bleach, etc? If you show there is space for all the needs of the buyer it's easier for them to envision making this their home! That being said… Use bins instead of the floor. Do you have a pole or table for laundry? Try to keep it clean or at least have laundry neatly folded or hung. Keep the tops of the appliances clean and clutter free!

Office Space/Rec Room: Organizing can not be stressed enough! People are always impressed when they see a general work area or play room that is neatly kept. It means you care about your home and surroundings. Overflowing shelves do not reflect useable space to them. Take the time to put away all personal papers! And any thing of value or importance. Take time to dust unused gym equipment or what ever you have in the Red Room. You want to give the appearance of usefulness, if you can not use it… this is the time to remove it… keep decluttering as you go!

Garage: *Honestly, I had a neighbor that referred to her garage as 'The Shed.' I once asked her why? "Why? Because, I can't remember ever using it to park the car… so, it's a shed attached to the house."*
We both laughed. But in truth…. Kathy was right… many people use a garage as a shed once they purchase the property.

However, when a Buyer is looking for a home they almost ALWAYS look at a garage to fit their car! I even had one Buyer not purchase several homes because the garage was not tall enough to park his full size pick-up truck! Even though at his present home he parked in the drive and would most likely do the same at the new home. He wanted the option of being able to park inside!

I realize decluttering a garage can be daunting! My eldest son use to go horseback riding at a horse farm in Stafford Virginia. One of my lasting memories of those summers was pulling up to an over flowing garage where they were no longer able to completely close. It would only shut to about six inches off the ground. The barn was always as neat as a pin… but the garage was another story! I told our grown children they have until the end of the summer to come get their memories from storage now that they're out of college. They are not yet all settled, but we have decided to stop being their free storage unit. We all use some place in our home to store 'stuff.' Now, that you are selling and moving is the time to ask yourself… does this 'stuff' we never look at go with us? Or do we get rid of it? If it helps, 'Take a Picture.' A picture is worth a Thousand Words. Take a photo of the mess and set it next to your bed so you can consider it overnight. In the morning look at the photo of your garage as it is… does the photo weigh you down? If so, it's time to let go. What can you donate? Sell? What must you keep? The rest throw away!

Leave behind the extra paint, wood trim, and ceramic tiles for the new homeowner. All those bicycles can be packed up or hung up on the walls. The broker toys you met to repair can now be thrown away.

NOTE:
To those Pet Owners... this is the time to tuck away their toys into a box. Keep their bowls and litter boxes, and beds neat and as much out of the way as possible.

Be Aware: Do not smoke in your house, or leave ashes and cigarette butts on the porch or in the garage! This is the time to empty ashtrays daily. An ex-smoker is 10x more sensitive to smoke than a Non-smoker! They will not buy a home with signs or smells of smoke! Smoking is a very quick way to De-Value your home investment!!

Recently: while showing homes we went into a lovely colonial. The buyers voiced an interest in the home until we opened the garage door and they inhaled a strong whiff of stale cigarette fumes. The home showed well, and was spotless. The garage was well maintained, no visible sign of smoking, but the smell was unmistakable and a definite deal killer.

Deep Cleaning: The White Glove Test is the Name of the Game!

If you are not able to do a through deep cleaning yourself... it is wise to Hirer a Cleaning Service to come do a Deep, Through Cleaning for you. And then you need to keep up with keeping the place in order while it's on the market. I can not stress enough how VITAL this one act can be!

*Recently, I was out showing homes to out of
Town Buyers. We went to see a home on a particular
Street. There was another down the road that had recently came on
the market. They asked to add that home to the list.
I went up and knocked on the door. A lady said that, 'yes, we could
see the house.'
Great!*

We entered. She left. The Master bedroom was a mess. But there was a crib in the corner so my clients said, 'no problem. It's understandable that the room is messy. They must be new parents.' As we were leaving a couple arrived. The husband was annoyed we were in the way of him entering his side of the garage. Worse, the wife gets out and starts screaming that we went in without permission. I explained we has another persons permission. She got on the phone with her agent.

The agent saw my message I sent when entering the house, but called to say the lady had a house keeping business and was upset she had left her own room a mess.
OK, don't embarrass or frighten potential buyers for your lack of preparedness.
Most excited buyers will overlook the mess because they surprised you. They will not over look an irate seller that is angry they are there. They do not want to buy a place from someone that is not ready to move.

Think about a used car you plan to trade in... You know you'll get more money for a professional quality cleaning on a car than one that shows signs of wear. So why not take the same effort in your home?

You want to Clean each room one at a time and include closets, nooks and built in bookshelves. Be meticulous, especially in common areas like the kitchen and bathrooms. Pay attention to any marks on the walls, stairs and carpets. Tighten the railings. Home Buyers will be opening cabinets, pantries and closets.

With that in mind you need to pay attention to:
Cobwebs in corners and on ceilings
Dust ceiling fans, lights, light fixtures and vents, room boilers or wall units
Dust or replace blinds and lampshades
Wash the walls, touch up where needed.
Clean all glass surface. If you're not good at cleaning windows and mirrors, television screens, etc... hirer someone who is. As a teenager a friend showed me that a newspaper was better at preventing window streaks than using a paper towel.

Polish wood work! Floors and cabinets!
Wipe down leather furniture. Steam cloth furniture.
Keep kitchen cabinets clean and organized.

BE SURE TO CLEAN all Appliances! Both in the kitchen and the
utility room! Hot Water Heaters are often overlooked by Sellers, and
never overlooked by Buyers.

Be sure to put away any unused appliance so that counter space is
kept clear! This makes a kitchen shine and gives a sense of space!
Be sure to clean sinks, toilets, tubs and showers, faucets and grout
lines, and the top of the hot water heater. Placing a toilet bowl cleaner
in the tank helps keep the toilet bowl sparkling and fresh.
Clean the window treatments even if you plan to take them with you.
If your blinds are old, and brittle this is a good time to replace them and
leave them for the buyers.
Clean the screens or take them out while showing.
Vacuum and shampoo carpets, and rugs.
Mop and if need be wax the floors throughly.

Focus — Kitchen and Baths:
We all agree... A Kitchen can sell a house, because it's the center of
a home. Undoubtedly, this is a place where friends and family gather.
That being said Buyers are looking for this room to be especially clear
of dirt, grime and smells like strong cooking odors or stinking trash.
Avoid unattractive smells by using an odor eliminator if you enjoy lots
of spices in your cooking. Keep the trash can emptied daily to cut
down on trash odors. Clean cabinet surfaces, appliance surfaces, etc.
after each use.

Bathrooms are more important than we think! When taking a photo of
a bathroom try to avoid photos of the toilet. Many people from other
countries find this offensive, especially if the toilet seat is up! So,
please be certain to lower the lid before leaving the house when you
are planning a showing.

It's really important to keep every bathroom clean and neat and odor
free while marketing your house for sale! Pick up kids tub toys and
stools and store them under the sink or in a corner out of the way.

Potential Buyers may give leeway to a slightly untidy child's room, but many will not enter a cluttered or dirty bathroom and this could cost you a sale.

Addressing the Guerrilla in the Room:
This is a very touchy subject that many Agents try to avoid, but must be addressed!

Pet Lovers Love, Love, Love their pets! Non-pet owners not so much.

Do Not limit the buyer pool by having your barking dog or overly friendly cat have the run of the house!

Be aware people have pet allergies. Pet dander, pet hair and odors are a turn-off to many buyers viewing experience.

> *It's an unnecessary distraction. The pets are not conveying with the house so please minimize contact with strangers by keeping them out of sight as much as possible. If possible take them out of the home, or relegated to the garage, basement or back yard or in a caged area for showings.*

Keep their dishes, bedding and toys, litter boxes clean and odor free.

Once The Deep Cleaning, Decluttered and Staged you are ready to List Your House for Sale!!!

Even with all the Internet Information and the Good Intensions of Friends and Family a Realtor is still your very best source of information. They can provide insight on how to sell your home quickly at the best price. There is a great deal to consider when setting the price. Pricing properly upfront and knowing the local market is a huge benefit in getting your home sold quickly. An Experienced Real Estate Professional will also have a great deal of negotiation skills you may not have.

Chapter 8

Help - Market Your Home

We all want to sell our property quickly for the most money. This book touches on options you have to help make that Goal a Reality! In previous chapters we have outlined some Do's and Don'ts to assist in getting your home sold fast for top dollar. Now, I would like to take a moment to highlight how price is determined and the significance of Market Value.

Despite whether the media says its a "Buyer's Market" or a "Seller's Market" it's really always in the Seller's control. Why? Homes are a necessity. The choice is whether to buy or rent. Renters on average pay more for a domicile than an owner will pay. That being said, 'Real Estate' is clearly a commodity. There are a variety of choices depending on location. When we discuss residential property in this book we are including: Single Family Detached Homes; Patio Homes, Townhomes, Duplexes; Condos, Mobile Homes on a Permanent Foundation, Modular Homes on permanent foundation; Homes with land, Homes in a Subdivision, Even City Apartments. We are not including Mobile homes, RV's or Timeshares. Even though these are "Homes" they are not conveyed the same way, and therefore should be covered in a separate book.

That being said now is the time to think about, 'What makes your house and property unique?' 'Do you remember why you chose this house above all others?' 'What do you LOVE most about your house?' 'What is one thing you would change?' See, every property is a different challenge because every property is somehow unique. Somehow you're able to go home every day to the right house rather than the same house around the corner. Something is different in your mind to you that sets it apart from all the other houses in the neighborhood. It's this uniqueness that makes selling homes off-a-store shelf difficult.

So, how does an Appraiser or Realtor come up with a Value? Your home's Value will be impacted by what Similar homes in the area (or if a rural setting, it may be a radius) have sold for in the past 3 to 12 months depending on the location of your property. In a city a Lender is going to be looking at the past 3 months. In rural or farm areas across the country it may be the Appraiser will have to look back 6 to 12 months. They may need 4 - 6 comparable instead of 3 comparable. An Appraiser is looking at LOCATION, Approximate distance from your property to the comparable. TIME, like I said 3 to 12 months back for most recent, similar sales. AGE, of your home vs the comparables. SIZE, both the above square footage of the house as well as the land it sits upon. Do you have the same number of bedrooms and bathrooms as the comparable? Is your house obsolete or common for the area? Anything that effects 'Marketability' should be addressed in the appraisal. Even with all of no one person or professional can guarantee the salability of your property over your neighbors property. Real Estate is not cut and dry!

In the end, YOU - Mr. & Mrs. Homeowner Ultimately Set the Asking Price of your Home. A Realtor simply supplies you with the available data to make an informed decision on the best price. An Appraiser may Support your price, but they are going off the data available for a small area and for a short window of time. Real Estate is a constant Practice. It changes constantly! This is why Part-Time Agents often have a difficult time with helping a homeowner set a good price. In today's competitive Online Marketing how do you figure out what is the best exposure for your property? Will Professional Photos help sell your house fast? Will online shoppers in your market even care if the photos are done by a professional or not? What Marketing Plan does the Realtor have? Do they allow you to help or have a say? Or do they take over and want you to stand aside? Are you good with standing aside?

Let's be Reasonable on the List Price. It's all negotiable from here on out!
As I have previously stated "Perception of Value drives the sale of Real Estate!

This is the place I want to take a moment to offer something to consider: Look at your preliminary Closing Cost Estimate Sheet from your Realtor. A knowledgable Agent will provide this sheet for you upfront. You'll see how much you are paying in commissions broken down to the Seller's Side and the Buyer's Side... when you consider an auction you should deduct the commission from your closing cost. Additionally, deduct the Buyer's Closing Cost Concessions. Add these numbers to your bottom line! Now, consider how much less your Reserve Price can be without these cost being paid by you! That is the number you would be happy with. How much more please would you be if it sells for more than your reserve?

I realize not all Realtors offer this alternative option to selling your home. If you're a farmer you may be very comfortable buying and selling your home and contents via an Auction. I say this because growing up in a farming community the Auction was a way of life. People bought and sold livestock, farm equipment, land, etc at an auction. As an adult living in urban areas I enjoyed going to 'Estate Sales' with friends.
Many of my contemporaries never imagined buying anything at an auction. We would have 'Silent Auctions' as a fund raiser. The more comfortable you are with auctions the more natural this process will be for you.

Actually, very few Realtors offer this option but sometimes the best option maybe an Auction. Auctions are not a bad thing! If you use a notable Real Estate Auction House with a following and proven track record they will often get more than your Reserved Price.

What is a *'Reserve Price?'* This is the bottom line you are willing to sell the property for. If your Reserve is not met you list it as a conventional sale with an agent. How does the Auction work? It depends on the company. I would use an Auctioneer that collects the premium from the Buyer. Additionally, many auctioneers want an up front Marketing fee. Make certain its something you can afford... do not go into debt for this Marketing Fee. As we are in the Technology World there are two Auction Options... the inexpensive Online Auction. Or the tried and true in person Auction. As this is your property this is not on the courthouse steps. This is held at the site of your property! Better yet, if you have furniture or outdoor equipment you want sold you can ask the Auctioneer if they'll sell that too. Most of the time they will do two separate auction... one for the content the other for the property. I've worked with other Auction Companies over the years... United Real Estate has one of the Top Auction Houses in the United States. They not only sell a good portion of auctions in the country they have one of the best Auction Schools too! Auctions are a viable tool to consider. It's always best to make informed decisions based on facts and knowledge. If you're curious I recommend attending a local auction prior to deciding it is right for you.

Regardless of what option you chose its important to price the property correctly. When it comes to real estate I can not stress enough the importance of LOCATION! It doesn't matter what type of real estate you are selling... commercial, industrial, farmland, or residential property Location is a big part of the VALUE. As the Property Owner its important to help your Realtor with the Perceived Value verses Market Value. If you and your Realtor are able to spin a big enough perception you can sell the property for more than the Market Value.

As a Seller, there are few things you should keep in mind:

• Your Sentiments have no dollar value. The more you pack up prior to Listing the easier it should be too *'let go.'* The more you let go the easier it will be to set a reasonable list price. It's very important to set a competitive price upfront. If you have to make regular price adjustments you may need to consider if you're creating the market or are you chasing the market.

- If you're reading this book I hope it means you're willing to set aside sentimentality. Buyers are looking for your motive to sell. They believe in, 'making an offer.' Many will be below your list price... will you be happy with that?

- Consider that updates and improvements may help sell a home quicker, but you will most likely not get a dollar for dollar sales price adjustments.

    Prime example: A swimming pool may cost $10,000 to $30,000 to install. It may provide the 'saleability' of your home, but it will not add enough tangible value to offset the cost.

    All too often I have seen swimming pools get filled in because they're to much work or they need a new liner.

    A whole house vac may add interest and help create a quick sale, however, it rarely adds a dollar for dollar sales increase.

    Example: Recently, I went on a Listing Appointment to a home that had 'Inoperable' Solar Panels on the roof. They were an eye sore. But to remove them met the Seller would need to replace the roof.

  Hearing that money was tight due to a long illness I didn't advise her to take them down. Instead, I gave her options. -A. Sell the house as is for $10,000 under market.
Or -B. Remove the panels and pay a roofer to replace the roof.
The Seller chose option B.
I believe it's your house until it's sold. I can show you what works, it's your ultimately your choice which way you go.

    In Contrast: Had they been Operational Solar Panels they would have truly added value to the home. They would have been a Marketing Feature as well as brought a bit hirer price as people see the long term energy benefits.

A fireplace adds value if there is room for the fireplace. I have seen people chose a home with an imitation fireplace over a similar home without a fireplace! A fireplace adds value!

Consider this: A fireplace, garage, deck have a designated space on an appraisal. That indicates they all add significant value.

I am presently working with a couple relocating to Virginia from New Jersey. They have commented every time we enter a home with approximately three thousand dollar sliding glass door with a bar or rail across them instead of seeing a deck to walk out on.
They wonder aloud each time: 'Why have the sliding glass doors if you don't have the money for the deck?'
Great question…. I don't have an answer for them. Clearly, it would have been wiser to go with a large window for light if no deck was going to be built.
I can only say… not all Builders think wisely. And too many buyers believe they will add the deck at a later date and later never came. Or they expected a sales person to 'Up sell' a deck to a prospective buyer.
Honestly, if no deck is going to be added at time of build it is better not to have the sliding glass doors. On re-sales there is no value to having a slider over a large window. In fact: if they have small children they will not buy a home with a slider with bars and no deck as it poses a risk factor.
Please use common sense when putting your home on the market.

Ask yourself: How much am I willing to invest to receive a better return? Do you need a new roof? A deck? Stairs to the basement? To help you sell this house?
Are these things you've put off and know you should have them done?

Then, please do them so that your house does not sit to long on the market. At present there is a 'pend-up-demand' for homes on the market. So, when I have listings that simply sit month after month and the Seller's ask, "Why?" I can take them out and show them the homes that have been sitting are just like theirs. Today's buyers want CLEAN, MOVE-IN READY HOMES. Or they are investors looking to offer low, do minimal work to sell high. So, if you do not have the money to make every repair at least invest in CLEANING and a FRESH COAT OF PAINT! I can not stress enough how much farther these to things will take you!

Chapter 9

A Picture is worth a 1,000 Words

Believe me: A picture is worth thousands of dollars when taken well. It can be the difference of a showing or no showing as 85% of today's real estate buyers begin on-line.

I have a new agent that was very zealous with his picture taking on his first few listings. He was certain he knew more than I did about marketing to people his own age.

You want an agent to take lots of pictures of your home. You also want an agent who weeds through their photos to only use the best shots when marketing your house. After the homes didn't sell in the first two weeks the agent and his clients came to blame me for the failing. I listened and then pointed out the fact they were well aware he was inexperienced and they did not want my help initially when offered. Now, that they were in my office I had to ask, 'Are you really ready for what I have to say?'

Fair enough. I gave them a list of items that needed taken care of before new pictures could be taken. I told them by making repairs after the house is listed will impact the sales amount as well as the time it will sit on the market. I reiterated they needed to control the things they can control and be aware there are negatives they can not control.

A Common Mistake that may stop a home from selling is how a picture is taken. It doesn't matter how expensive the camera is if the photographer has no knowledge of lighting. You will not achieve a good photo in the dark.

A.

B.

Lighting and angles play a big part of Real Estate. For this reason, some Realtors take their own shots while others prefer to pay a professional to take the photos. Taking photos of property is far different than taking photos of people. Property is perspective and lighting. Outside photos make need to be taken a various times of the day to get it just right. In addition to lighting a photographer must consider 'angles.'

A.

B.

Which of these photos do you find more appealing?

Not all Photographers are skilled at taking professional photos of buildings. And not all Agents are skilled at taking a professional, quality photo. That's why some real estate companies insist on the Seller hiring a professional photographer. A skilled photographer will bring out the best in a home via photographs.

Just as having your property listed without a photo is like going fishing without a pole so too is loading a bunch of bad photos of your home online. Remember: I said, todays buyer is looking for CLEAN, MOVE-IN READY HOMES. If your photos reflect clutter, trash outside or unmade beds these buyers are going to skip going to that home.

Your on-line photos are your enticement to the buyers. Make this bit of Marketing your very best! Imagine it is your One Shot to make a Great First Impression! Photos convince interest to see more. Offer the buyer something no one else is offering. It may be insignificant to you, but it may seal the deal for the home buyer.

Keep in mind… a Buyer is looking for an incentive. Your photos are that initial incentive. Entice them to come and see more!

In addition to the photos what makes your house special? Do you have a whole house vacuum? Are you willing to pre-pay the real estate taxes for the next year? Does your house have more 'useable' land than the neighbors?

Whatever makes your home unique is the draw that a Realtor can use to market your home to stand out against the competition.

Be sure to ask your agent: 'How will you market my home?'
Do they have a Marketing Plan? Do they share with you a 'Marketing Calendar?' Do they make a slide presentation you can access to share with people you know? If you're excited to sell your home all the people you know will be excited to sell your home and that excitement will bring you buyers.

Chapter 10

Formula's sell homes in
3 steps

As humans comfortable in a situation or home we become complacent. When we are complacent we often over look the small details that make a big difference!

Consider how small details can make a big difference. Here are a few examples I see over an over again.

- Home has been on the market for over ten months. Time to refresh and Sell it in the next 45 days! Changing agents doesn't always get the job done!

- Home was listed with another agent for six months. They put it in the MLS and made listing fliers. Little else. No showings. We took the listing. New photos, a Brokers Open and the home sold in 45 days.

- Home was one the market for 18 months with two other agents. It had not sold. I Listed it and sold the home in 75 days. The owners were thrilled.

- Home was in poor shape. The family had a tragic story that left them broke. They needed to sell for what was owed. I took the listing and had it 'under contract,' in 4 days!

These are just a few examples of what can be done in a few basic steps.

#1. Solve the Problem. What is holding back the sale?
It may be hard to believe, but Price is not always the answer to the problem. Recently, I had 2 different home buyers I was working with tell me they went to an advertised "Open House" and the home was not open. One told me they arrived behind three other potential buyers. They all got out of their cars and chatted thinking perhaps the agent was simply running late.

I went with a third buyer to a home to find no Agent. Upon texting the agent he said he changed the Open House date to the following weekend and gave me a code to show it.

Not for nothing, but you need to check up on vacant homes to see that the agent you hired is following through on their marketing promises to you.

Truthfully: Agents are human. Some are not good agents. Some simply get sick or have personal issues that get in the way, and do not reach out to others for help.

The best agents are Problem Solvers. They solve your problems and the house sells.

#2. Marketing Improvements. I can not stress enough the value of a good picture verses and Excellent picture. Sometimes it pays to have a professional picture…. When selling a house… its one of those times.

A great agent provides an "In depth Marketing Analysis." This Analysis helps identify marketing opportunities. Understanding your community and customizing a marketing plan around those specifics will help your home sell even if you don't quite understand how.

Example: If you live in an area where 70% of the median homes have two college graduates as the bread winners and children between 14 - 24 a toddler gym in the back yard isn't going to necessarily help your home sell as much as a fire pit and koi pond would.

Creating a draw whether inside or out requires well lit photos. Taking the time to have photos done right can make even a dull home sell quickly!

#3. Improve the showing appearance of your home. Staging can make or break a home sale deal. There is not doubt.... 'A STAGED HOME will increase sales by 10% to 15%.

Do you know why Short Sales are often a "Bargain" price?
When I walk into most short sales I can immediately tell there's something wrong in the house hold. The place is often cluttered and in need of repair. They may be stinky, and an overall depressed feel. They are often not much of a deal for the buyer... but they are an opportunity for the buyer to create a place for themselves. Those that buy a Short Sale or Foreclosed home know they are buying under market price because they need repairs and they are willing to spend on the repairs to achieve their dreams.

Recently, and acquaintance who is down on her luck wanted to sell her townhome. She admitted it needed about $5,000 in repairs, but she didn't have the money to make those repairs. Additionally, she was behind in her mortgage. OK, you can sell "As Is" for below the market by $5,000 to $10,000 to make up for the needed repairs and still have a little for yourself after the mortgage is paid off.

She was relieved... until she spent the weekend with relatives in Washington DC. She called me up on Monday and suggested listing the home "As Is" for $20,000 over the market because her cousin suggested it. I asked her, "Why do that? What would entice a buyer to buy your home "as is" for more than the market would bare?" Her reply was because her cousin said so. "OK, so you want to chase the market when you have no time to chase it instead of being ahead of the game. Why would I want to help you do that by listing at an unrealistic price?" She had no answer for that.

In today's market if your home doesn't sell in a specific amount of time Buyers assume there is something WRONG with the home that goes beyond price. Overpricing is a bad idea.....even if you've agreed to regular price changes. If you're making a price adjustment in the first 10 days then you did not price your home correctly in the beginning and the agent is smart enough to have foreseen the need to come down in price to match the market.

Yesterday, I was showing homes to a girlfriend and her husband. Three homes, two were vacant. All priced about the same. The first vacant home was spotless and beautiful! It had been regularly 'aired' and showed well with beautiful hardwood floors throughout. The second home smelled 'musty,' the carpet was in good shape, but old feeling. The house was clean, but lacked a sense of comfort because it was musty and dated. The third house had someone staying in a guest room. It was clean and very manly throughout.

What I realized while listening to my friends as they walked through these three homes all listed for about half a million dollars was simply this: *Sometimes it's the little things that kill a deal.*
The first house will sell much quicker than the other two.
Do you know why?

1. As I said, Home one was spotless, had frequently been 'aired' and had beautiful hardwood floors. - Remember I said most of todays buyers are looking for 'move-in ready.' This house is 'MOVE-IN READY. Unless the Home Inspector finds something major the home will sell.
2. House number 2 'smelled musty.' There were cobwebs in the garage. If an Agent has a vacant house it would be to everyones benefit to either go open it for an hour once a week. Put in air fresheners, and take a broom to clean out cobwebs or have the sellers line up a cleaning service to do this on a weekly bases. This is one reasons hiring a Local Realtor is a benefit to the Seller. If the Realtor is more than 45 minutes away they are most likely not going to be willing to go above and beyond to get the home sold.

3. The benefit of a Realtor in home number 3 maybe to encourage the person in the guest room to keep everything tidy. To go in before a showing to add a touch like fresh flowers in the kitchen, or the a room freshener plug in. Even providing a roll of cookie dough from the grocery store for him to pop in the oven on Saturday morning to leave that lingering aroma for a showing on Saturday afternoon.

Small touches often make an amazingly successful marketing that the average agent doesn't do.

Sometimes you have a problem beyond your control. Like you live on gravel road with a common maintenance agreement with the neighbors and they don't want you to sell. OK, you can still make your home attractive and with CURB APPEAL. That may mean eliminating unnecessary vehicles from your driveway and yard. Power washing the front of your home. Adding colorful cushions to your outdoor furniture on the patio, etc. There are a number of little touches your Realtor may suggest that will offset the poorly maintained gravel road leading up to the house.

A practiced Professional Realtor has infinite knowledge to help you sell your home at a realistic, marketable price. It's your job to really listen to what they are saying. If you want your home to sell in a reasonable amount of time listen to what they have to say. If you disagree sit down with them and see if there is an alternative game plan. Ultimately, your house will not sell without your cooperation.

Why go with a Local Professional in today's "Help me Sell" online market?

You, as a Home Seller, may believe you know as much as a professional that has spent time and money to learn a trade where they are Licensed and governed by their state as to what they can and can not do. A licensed Professional will keep you out of marketing trouble by honoring the rules of their profession that your may not even have considered until you find yourself in trouble.

As a Home Seller, you can bombard social media, and every website you can think of. You can drive your friends and family crazy by begging their assistance in putting up flyers on bulletin boards all over the area, in car windows at parking lots, etc.

Is Time not a valuable commodity to you? It is to me. As you are not a professional Realtor or Marketeer do you know if all your efforts are worthy of the time invested? Are they worth the inconvenience you have imposed on friends and family?

If being a Licensed Realtor was so easy that you believe you could do a better job than any agent I doubt that 85% of those agents obtaining their license today would agree with you. Because after the first 2 years in real estate less than 15% of those that thought they knew what they were getting into re-new their license. That tells me that selling real estate is a lot more difficult than most agents let on. There is a lot more to selling a house than putting the sign in the yard and a lockbox on the door!

If less than 15% of new agents renew their licenses don't you believe that a great Realtor knows what sells better than you do?
Do you care if the potential buyers is interested in your photos or skips your home because of poor photos? Are you willing to listen and act on the words of the professional? Because the Seller you either work with a Realtor and sell your home quickly, or you work against them and sit and wonder why. The blame is ultimate not with the Realtor but with yourself because of the choices you made.

A Great Home can not Sell Itself.
Marketing is needed.

As a Realtor, I am not going to argue as to whether or not I have more experience in marketing and selling than you do. I know how to Showcase your home. I go through it inside and out with you before putting that sign in the yard. I point out things you need to do. If you want to tell me you know more than me... Fine. Your home will sit and be a reflection to your infinitely greater knowledge than mine. That's OK with me. Is it OK with you?

I'm an impartial observer telling you what I see needs to change for the consumer you wish to attract. You are bias and therefore blind to some of the little details that a licensed professional Realtor will see and mention to you. Please do not take their suggestions lightly, these small points often impact the sales price of your home significantly!

When a builder begins construction on a home they begin with a blueprint. Then comes the foundation. Without a properly constructed foundation no house will stand for any length of time. In the Same way when you're ready to sell your home you need a marketing strategy that both you and your agent agree too.

Rushing off to post an ad for your home on Facebook or other social media may do little good if the photos show a mess in the front yard or a lawn that needs mowed. Worse yet, it may show more of what's in your neighbors garage than the front of your house.
You may have words in the description that do not meet Fair Housing Laws.

A true Real Estate Professional knows the basic strategies are the foundation of any successful marketing plan to sell your house.

Ready to give me a call? I have a network of professional Realtors throughout the country that help me help you in your specific area. Let me show you the strategies for marketing your home that will bring the perfect buyer.

Chapter 11

Negotiation comes with Experience

Let's be honest, there is a place for Realtors in today's marketplace. Yes, the internet changes the playing field with the 'Buy Me' Button. Or Companies like Amazon joining forces with Real Estate Firms to undercut other Realtors commissions by offer incentives that I may not be able to compete with. That's the tool of marketing via a big fish in a small pond.

By choosing that route you cheat yourself out of going with experience and sincerity vs a number cruncher out to make a dollar without concern for repeat business or referrals.

C'est la vie! All too often I hear people complain during or after the sale of their property. In all honesty, your agent can only do so much without your say so. You are ultimately in the driver's seat. If you are not please with the agent you have... you have the right to fire them up until you have a ratified contract in place. You need to do it in writing in most states.
Take the time to interview others and go with someone you like.

Real Estate is an interactive business. A good Realtor is someone you could see yourself as becoming 'friends' with. Take the time to make a good choice.

When you're working as a team member with your Realtor they will go to bat for you. Those subtle negotiations not just over price, but what may be left behind by you for the buyer may come into play. There are other negotiations you may not see, like a discount for the termite test or home warranty by using an affiliate partner. Or the Realtor helping you negotiate better prices for Home Inspection repair items.

I have worked with investors over the years who act as if they have more
Knowledge than I do about well or septic, or repairs.
Perhaps they do. I confess, I am minimally knowledgable in regards to
Well & septics. Some Realtors have no knowledge at all.
Those agents should not work in an area where Well/Septic are common
Unless they are working with an experienced agent. - but they will
If you do not specifically ask if they have experience.
I do not need to be an expert in well and septics as
I am not installing them.

PLEASE BE AWARE: I should understand how a septic system works, even though I need not know how to repair them. I should be aware there are different kinds, And what those differences are and how they impact my client And how they impact the transaction.

Recently, I had an trailer investor that believed I needed to know the Specific parts of a Septic System and how to properly install it. No, that is not a Realtor's place. A Realtor should know all the components of a system. We should advise our clients to get them inspected by a Professional In that field. As a Realtor, I should know there are several ways to inspect a septic system, and advise a client as to which inspection works best and why. For the most part I suggest a walk-over inspection as excavating may damage a system. However, there are times when an excavation is the best course of action. I need to be aware of the difference so that I can make proper recommendations to my clients. As I am not a professional in that field, I recommend, I do not insist. Someone with the proper knowledge will see if something is not Installed correctly and if any component needs repaired or Replaced.

I am not an Accountant. Yet, I should be knowledgable enough with my Business taxes to know that they are being properly prepared.
If I am working with an Investor I should understand ROI.
I should be interested and knowledgeable enough on what I can And can not deduct from my taxes as a business owner, and an investor myself.
That being said, I am not a CPA and therefore, I am not Knowledgable enough to give you tax council on real estate matters.
I do have referrals to people that can advise you for those questions.

A few years ago, a Large Northern Virginia Real Estate 'Team' took a Listing in Spotsylvania that had a propane tank for fuel.
Here is where knowledge and negotiation experience from an knowledgeable Realtor
Comes in handy.
That 'Team' was unfamiliar with propane tanks.
They told the Seller's they needed to Top off the Propane tank for the buyers. (Remember: this Team Listed the Property. They should have been looking out for the Seller's Interest)
The Seller's Topped off the Propane Tank. This cost several hundreds of dollars, depending on market rate.
I was familiar with propane tanks, as I am from the area. When looking at the property the buyers
Asked about propane so I happened to look and see that the tank was full.
I wrote the contract asking whether or not the tanks were leased or owned. (I was careful not to mention the propane inside)
I offered no "pro-ration" to the Seller.
The Seller's Agent provided the Information I requested without asking for a 'Pro-ration' of propane within the tank.

The house went to closing, keys were handed over.
A week later the Listing "Team's" Representative called me looking for The Pro-ration. I said, "Thank you for the Gift."
The Team Representative laughed. "Ya, right. My Seller is looking for the Pro-Ration."
Here was a sore spot for that agent: "You didn't ask for a Pro-ration,"

I responded. "Therefore, you do not get a 'Pro-ration."
Needless to say
The Agent was irate. But that is part of negotiation.
Sometimes the best negotiation is playing close to the vest.
That's my job... to get the Best Deal for My Client... regardless
Of what side I am working.
This is one reason I prefer not to do Dual.
In a Dual situation, I have no ability to negotiate.

Back to my investor with the Septic issue. In Virginia homes are sold
"As Is," unless You Ask for More.

This Investor thought he knew more than me. I advised him to get a
Home Inspection. He chose not to because he knew all he needed to
know.
OK, guess what... if you know... you are accepting the property 'as is'
you can not then ask for an escrow for 90 days after.
Had you done a 'Home Inspection' you would have more negotiation
power.

In addition to having waived the Home Inspection, this was a Cash
Purchase. Cash is not King when you skip Due Diligence.
This Investor believed they did not need due diligence.

Even though he refused the 'Home Inspection' I told him the Well and
Septic Inspections and Termite Inspection were still required. On a
CASH deal the Buyer
Can waive these as well, but if the Seller is paying why not
Get them done?

He accepted this small delay in closing, and was happy he had when
he realized that the Septic needed a repair. And I had allocated a
basic cost for repair and wrote it into the Septic Addendum.

However, once the repair of one component on a septic was done he
wanted to Escrow an amount for three months after the closing to
ensure the entire septic system would work

He forgot he had agreed to an 'As Is, Cash Offer' without a Home
Inspection or removing the 'As Is' clause of the contract.
If he would like to re-negotiate the whole contract we could ask for
An additional escrow. But that is not what he was willing to do.

Part of negotiation is knowing the perimeters and being willing to
Allow them to be changed.

As a Realtor working with a Seller, I am negotiating on your behalf
to sell your home at not only the best price but also the best situation
for you to achieve your goals.

If you receive a Full Price Offer, but the buyer wishes to delay for the
settlement for three months until their home sells negotiations may be
needed. Or you may accept a lower contract price contract that is
desires to close in thirty days. By presenting both options to you and
having a conversation I have negotiated contracts with my clients over
all best interest is maintained.

Sometimes Seller's Believe they are skilled Negotiators. Great,
do you have the time to meet with every prospective buyer and buyer's
agent.
If the home has not sold in eight months and you've moved from the
area are you able to carry a 'Vacant' home indefinitely?

Now, you've become a "Motivated Seller" who may or may not have
the time or other resources to really choose a good agent to sell your
home.

Are you able to arrange for 'Up keep' from your new location or did
you chose a Realtor that will manage that aspect for you?

Are you feeling 'stressed' yet?

Do you have a job that allows for the phone time and emotional
energy you need to manage selling your house?

Is your job sympathetic to you're dealing with issues that arise because you choose not to use a Realtor?

So, you list with a Realtor. That Realtor advertises you as "Motivated Seller's" because you have already moved and you home is vacant. You've confided that you are stretching things to maintain two households.

A Contract Offer comes in from a potential Buyer. They love your house… it's perfect for them! In fact, the wife wrote you a letter and insisted the agent add it to the Contract Offer. However, they have offered 10% under your list price and are asking you to pay 4% of their closing cost.

This is a skilled buyer's negotiator. You can bet this Buyer's Agent researched the home and knows you moved out three months ago after trying to sell the home on For Sale By Owner for five months. He's looked you up on Facebook and other social media and knows you need to sell your home. He knows you are unhappy with your agent, but as you moved you don't dare switch this far into the game.

Guess who has the upper hand?
Exactly, by spouting off on social media you showed your hand and painted your Listing Agent into a corner.

Moral of this story: When selling a house please, please, please refrain from talking to everyone you know about the situation. Please refrain from posting on social media every issue that arises. In today's market… you may sink your own ship with the cannon fired in the wrong direction.

In this instance the Buyer negotiated $40,900 below asking price plus another $12,270 in closing cost as the Listing Agent was able to negotiate the Seller's Closing Contributions from 4% to 3%, but as this was the Seller's first offer in 9 months and they were happy to take the price the Buyer offered rather than countering to a higher price.

Mr. Seller was so stressed by the time this contract came in they didn't even ask the Buyer to split the difference.
Overall Americans are not accustom to negotiating or haggling on prices.

Many Car Dealers even advertise a "NO Haggle Price." So why would you think differently on selling your house?

Chapter 12

Negotiation Nuggets

As a Certified Negotiations Expert I actually took several full day classes to learn the lessons I knew as a child attending Live Stock Auctions.

#1. Have an Idea of Value or Price before stepping into the ring.
What? Yes, know what something is going for when it's brand new or at the open market before bidding at an auction. The same applies to real estate. Do not expect your castle to sell for the same price as the Newly Built home down the street.

Realize: what's the motivation? Sometimes we enter bidding wars on a property and get carried away by a competitive spirit. It's important to realize negotiation isn't always about price alone. I recently showed 2 homes for sale side by side. The one on the corner was listed for $50,000 more than the other. The difference... the corner lot. The outward appearance of a 4 car garage, which was now a 2 small car garage and 'Man Cave' on the inside. My client liked the house next door better, and it was not simply the difference in price. It was style.

When dealing with Bank Foreclosures they always ask: Is this buyer going to occupy or not occupy?

And: If the Investor wins the bid they often will require their contract be signed which may state 'this investor agrees to hold this property for twelve months prior to re-selling.'
What?
Yes, that is right. Banks have stipulations for buying their "as is" foreclosed homes.

As a 'Regular Sale' it is a RESPA Violation to stipulate how long the buyer keeps possession of the property you are selling. It may be a Fair Housing Violation to stipulate who may and may not purchase the home.

#2. Know your opponents motivation. Why do the Buyers like this house?

Where are they moving from? You may not ever know the answer to this question, but you can take the time to 'preview' the homes you believe you are competing with. Take the time to look at a newly built home in your area. Take the time to look at one or two homes for sale in your neighborhood because they will give you insight and ideas for staging your property.

How does my house compare to the house down the street in another subdivision? If you check out these homes with me or another Realtor, you'll be able to answer this question.

If you want to know 'Market Value' look up "Open Houses" in your neighborhood and start checking out the competition.

Are there new homes being built in your area? If so, are they selling for more or less than you're asking for your home?

If it's more, and it should be, because construction cost change over time. Take the time to go find out what features or styles today are similar to your property's features and style.

If the new homes are less than yours… what's the difference? Is it lot size? House size? A change such as no garage or deck that would cause a lower price point. Does this mean the people looking in your neighborhood may not be able to afford your larger home? Or that they may not want a large home. If that is the case, how is your Realtor going to market your large home in a changing market?

Notable qualities? You have established flower beds, mature trees for more privacy. A large yard, a wooden privacy fence. A garage and large deck. Be sure these features that sets you apart from the lower priced homes stands out.

Or do you need to realistically lower your price to be below the new home price? Are you able to objectively see that your home is not superior to the new homes being built in your area? This is why a Listing Realtor is so beneficial. It is often very hard for people to be objective when it comes to their home.

Are there unique features to your subdivision, community or town that make it more desirable?

For Example: Is your home in a Country Club neighborhood? Or on a Golf Course?
I live in Virginia Wine Country, making my house more desirable than a home just five miles down the road in another county. Is your house located in a Great School System vs a Fair School System. You may send your children to private school, so it has never mattered to you, but now that you are selling your home … this matters.

#3. I know I mentioned this in the last chapter… but this is REALLY IMPORTANT! Do you Talk Too Much?

When Negotiating… don't share your life story as the Seller of the property with the Buyer or their agent! That Agent doesn't work for you and may use the information to get a better deal for their client! That's their JOB!

Rarely do I do DUAL AGENCY because as a DUAL AGENT I can not possible negotiate on either parties behalf. Worse yet, anything you share with me I must share with the other party!

All to often people forget who they are talking too. The Buyer is usually Not your Friend or Family Member. They do not know you! So, stop sharing with them as if they do!

I sold a home that was owned by a daughter and her parents. The daughter was so angry that she walked out of the closing because her father chatted with the buyers and gave away all the lawn equipment in the shed she was planning to take to her new home!

Today's buyers are looking up what you owe on your house. Some even have in their minds how much you should make over and above what you purchased it for or what you presently owe! They judge the value of your home based on your debt against the house. I never said it was 'right thinking' I am simply the messenger!

They may also know if you are current or have been listed as a 'Pre-Foreclosure' or if your house is marketed as a 'Potential Short Sale'. As a 'Potential Short Sale' they realize their offer price makes a difference as to whether they are working with you or with your lender. There is so much out there on the internet today that is public knowledge. Worse yet, you are out there on Social Media often divulging way too much information about yourselves and your home. It makes my job challenging when it comes to negotiation.

#4. Showing your hand too soon. What does that mean?
I had a Seller call me to sell her home. She was an older acquaintance. I went out and gave her ideas to get a better price. "No. I want to sell as is."
"OK," I said, "there have not been any recent sales in this neighborhood for a year. I looked around and came up with a narrow range.

She thought her home 'as is' was worth more. So, we both called Investors we knew to come out to tour the house. Not one offered anywhere close to my lowest number in the range. She agreed to list the house but refused to clean up. Keep in mind I have said repeatedly in this book BUYERS WANT TO SEE A SPOTLESS WELL MAINTAINED HOME.

But in the end, it is your property. I can advise you on what you should do. How you should stage the home. What should be repaired. The best price you should start out with. In the end... it's your property, and your decision.

This lovely lady wanted out without effort. She was comfortable with the list price, as it was higher than any of the investors had offered, even after a few asked to purchase some of the furniture.

To help her get her price, I cleaned a disgusting mess in the bonus room, and with the help of my girls made a path in a bedroom suite that I was not able to enter upon first seeing the house.

After accepting an offer from multiple contracts at an 'As Is' price and agreeing to repair a water leak in the upstair bathroom a neighbor listed their smaller, pristine house for $20,000 more. That house was not as lovely as my clients. My listing was a brick, custom built home. The neighbor had a cookie cutter colonial that was smaller, but it sold for $20,000 more due to the fact it was spotlessly clean and well staged!

Of course my Seller lamented after the fact. As my girls and I had spent hours cleaning her house I looked at her and flatly reminded her that she had refused my offer of a "Professional Cleaning Service" coming to the house to clean. Instead, she used the cleaning lady she had for years and my girls and I. She refused to declutter until there was a contract in place where they stated they wanted the attic emptied. Rather than having a professional do repairs her husband who was no carpenter had made repairs that didn't quite work. When you're selling a home for $400,000 and up you should have a professional make repairs even if it hurts your spouse's feelings.

Yes, Janet could have gotten $30,000 more with a little effort on her part, up front. Mind you when she initially called me in February I told her flat out... 'You love your house. You've been there 25 years. Think about what you're willing to clear out and if you truly want to sell and call me back in a month.' I am paid by commission... I only get paid when I sell something. I make money by listing a house for sale, not by talking someone out of selling. Yet, I listen to people and frequently ask them, 'is this what you really want?' Or 'Will you be happy making this move?'
Why do I ask these questions? People my age and older often have a 'change of heart.' And when they do change their mind look out! All that anger about their changed decision after making a written agreement is directed at the person helping them... their Realtor. Rather than take the backlash of their fickleness I ask tough questions to be certain we are on the same page. Then, when they get mad down the road, or after the fact...

I have several conversations to refer to, that confirms I did what they paid me to do… Sell their house FAST so they could move on!

 # 5. Getting out of your own way! When negotiating it's like bidding at an auction. Be sure you keep your Goal in Mind. Remember; you want to sell your home in a timely fashion at a good price. When negotiating with a prospective buyer or two… keep your goal in mind!

I have a lovely listing on a poorly maintained dirt road. They received a low ball offer on their home; I recommended countering back. The Seller was too offended. He wanted to simply tell the Buyer not interested. "I understand you are insulted, but a bird in hand is better than a bunch in the bush."

The Seller shook his head. "No. This offer isn't worth considering." A month later the same buyer came back with a lower offer than the first time. It was an investor who was betting on the Seller's being desperate. They were not desperate however, the Buyer had failed to do his due diligence.

I have seen these investor buyers with big egos. They imagine they are great negotiators and take advantage of the desperation of others. From experience, these buyers are often willing to pay more than their initial offer price. They are looking for a Seller that can see past their anger at being insulted with a low offer. For those who preserve and open negotiations they will come up with a better price. The majority of Sellers loose sight of their goal and feel satisfied telling a potential buyer to take their low offer and kiss off. I always recommend that the Seller's I work with acknowledge every offer. If it is a substantially low offer at least open negotiations by countering back… even if it's only a few thousand off the List Price.

 # 6. Additionally, I suggested the Seller make a response as time is of the essence. Meaning they counter the low ball offer with a higher sales price as a deal that the buyer must respond to in the next 24 hours.

Example: Seller Mark has his home listed for $560,000.00 Investor Buyer Dill offered a low ball figure of $360,000.00. I suggested Seller Mark counter offer Investor Buyer Dill a sales price of $558,000.00 if accepted in the next 24 hours to close in thirty days or forfeit the earnest money deposit.

Seller Mark didn't see the value of countering at all. I suggested they had some interest or they would not have written an offer at all.

When any offer is in writing I content there is some amount of sincere interest. Why not push to see how much interest that is. If it brings you a price you can live with why not make the effort? Research your potential buyer. Perhaps you'll find out something that can be used to come to an agreeable sales price.

Chapter 13

Negotiation is a Tool

If you took basic Business Courses in High School you heard of **KISS Formula**: _Keep It Simple Stupid_. _Simple Negotiations_ often follow this formula. How does this apply to selling a home?

You have a goal... You want to be in the property Selling Business. Like most people you want this to be a Short Term employment much like a contract job. You began by giving your property a through Cleaning! Then you spruced up the place inside and out to give it some appeal to Home Buyers.

Now, you seek potential buyers to come and view your home. This is where the excitement builds and voila... you have an offer! Suddenly, all your efforts become realized.. Are you ready to move on this offer?

Selling your house is like purchasing a home for the very first time! It's one of the biggest investments most people ever make. This is an incredibly important financial decision as well as often a life changing moment emotionally. No, sweat, especially if you're working with a skilled professional Realtor. They, understand what you're going through. They have walked you through the steps to prepare you for this very moment.

It is true, the more money you make with this sale the better off you'll be. But by now you should have an honest idea of the value of your home as it is. This is a time to be realistic and not greedy. Remember Jane? Jane wanted her house sold, 'as is.' Even when some one purchases a house "as is" you will move out personal possessions before the closing of the transaction. In the offer Jane accepted the buyers actually put in that the 'attic had to be emptied and swept.' This attic was very large it was over a two and half car garage. Additionally, it was full of cast away toys and literally bags of trash and twenty years of paperwork from her business! When it was emptied I couldn't believe how large it seemed! After Jane saw the home cleaned up and emptied of all her furniture and personal stuff for new owners to move in she knew she could have gotten more if she had made an 'Effort.' Suddenly, she was angry with herself. This had been her dream home, she had helped design it and somewhere along the way she had let all the stuff in her life get the best of this beautiful home! Now, someone else would be able to restore it to its original glory.

I want every Seller I work with to come away with less debt and stress. When we're young we're full of energy and capable of maintaining a home a farm, where we chose to live. As we age, sometimes time works against our bodies and we are no longer able to maintain our home as we once did. Sometimes by the time we decide to sell, like Jane, the house has gotten the best of us. We are no longer able to keep it as we once did. With Jane's failing health she didn't have the 'energy' required to maintain a large home. When she hired people to help, their help was not sufficient to keep it as well maintained as Jane had maintained it in the past.

I want you to feel you made an informed decision in how much effort you put into the sale and marketing to come away with a fair price to you.

With each contract there is a need for some negotiations. Sometimes the 'Make me Sell' Button on the internet does not give you the best option. Who is looking out for your interest in this transaction? Who is covering your paperwork to ensure there is no backlash in the months after the closing?

I ask these questions from experience. A local Real Estate Investor believes in wearing down a Seller. He initially makes an offer typically of 70% of the list price. A HUGE MISTAKE most sellers make is ignoring low offers. I encourage my sellers to engage in negotiations even with a low offer. Most do not want to. This Investor will wait a month or two for a property they have interest in. If it doesn't sell they will come back with an even 'Lower' Offer! This investor was willing to pay more in the first offer. But when the Seller doesn't respond then he figures he can wait them out and get an even better price! As this method has worked in the past he will continue to use it.

For a Seller this low-offer tactic may be insulting. You've worked hard to beautify your property to make it attractive for a potential buyer. You've opened you house to potential buyers.

You've come to me for ideas, support and direction in the process of getting your home 'SOLD.' I am here to walk with you through one of the most important financial decisions of your life!

Sometimes having an impartial advocate enables you to get the best price for your home even from a low-ball investor. Let's work together and made this deal a reality!

When you work with a Professional Realtor that supplies a 'Seller Net Sheet,' that same Realtor will generally include Buyer Closing Cost reasonable to the area. In our area it's generally 3-4% of the sales price. When dealing with a Cash Buyer these Closing Cost are often not requested by the Buyer... so, this should be reflected in the bottom line. If you're not paying their cost out of your proceeds you may be willing to accept a lower 'Sales Price' to reflect this amount.

Many Buyer's in today's market are putting down little or nothing and need to scrap together funds to come up with the closing cost. If your Realtor sat with you prior to Listing and reviewed your chosen List Price by providing a Seller's Net Sheet then on that form you already built in 2-4% of Buyer's Closing Cost. Meaning even though you're paying their closing cost at the Closing Table, you've already allotted funds for that from your bottom line.

So, in essence the Buyer is actually paying those cost with an increased Sales Price.

Let me show you what I mean: Say you List your home for $250,000.00
The Buyer is looking for 3% in Closing Cost =   7,500.00
You essentially lowered the net proceeds to you as if you were selling
your home for $242,500.00

So, if an Investor makes an offer of $175,000.00 rather than say, "No, that offer is just too low; it would be better to allow me to counter back to the Investor with an offer of $246,000.00. This number is more than you would accept with the 3% in closing cost, and offers a reference point to the potential Buyer that says you believe your property is competitively priced.

SELLER'S ESTIMATED COSTS OF SETTLEMENT

PROPERTY:

TYPE OF FINANCING				
SALES PRICE		$	$	$
AMOUNT FINANCED				

ITEM	HOW COMPUTED			
Pre-rata interest on Existing Loan(s)	Interest Rate x Loan Balance ÷ by 365 x Number of Days; Prior Last Payment to the Settlement Date x 12 Days (See footnote regarding FHA loan payoff)**			
Prepayment Penalty	Check with Existing Lender	$	$	$
Estimated Payoff 1st Trust	Principal Balance	$	$	$
Estimated Payoff 2nd Trust	Principal Balance	$	$	$
Seller's Contribution to Purchaser's Closing Cost (if any)	As per Sales Contract			
Seller Paid Lender Fees	$800 - $900 (VA & FHA)	$	$	$
Prorated City/County Property Taxes/Assessments		$	$	$
Unpaid HOA/Condo/Coop Dues or Special Assessments				
Other Prorated Taxes		$	$	$
Other Liens		$	$	$
Brokerage & Financing				
Listing Company Compensation		$	$	$
Selling Company Compensation		$	$	$
Other		$	$	$
Closing				
Settlement Fee or Closing Fee	$250 - $600	$	$	$
Deed Preparation Fee	$100 - $300	$	$	$
Release of Liens/Trusts	Average $100 per Release	$	$	$
Other (power of attorney, etc.)		$	$	$
Miscellaneous (if applic.)				
Recording Releases	$41-49 per Release	$	$	$
Grantors Tax	$1.00 per $1,000 of Sales Price or assessed value (whichever is greater), rounded to next highest $500. OR if Loan is Assumed, $1.00 per $1,000 Above Principal Balance			
Regional WMATA Capital Fee (applicable in Alexandria City, Arlington, Fairfax, Loudoun and Prince William Counties and all cities contained within)	$1.80 per $1,000 of Sales Price or assessed value (whichever is greater), rounded to the next highest $100. OR if Loan is Assumed, $1.80 per $1,000 Above Principal Balance			
Pest inspection		$	$	$
Home Warranty	$325 - $800+	$	$	$
Well & Septic Inspection		$	$	$
Other Inspection		$	$	$
Repairs		$	$	$
HOA/Condo/Coop Disclosure	$100 - $500 per Association (POC*)	$	$	$
Other		$	$	$
Total Estimated Cost of Settlement		$	$	$

Sales Price		$	$	$
LESS: Total Estimated Cost of Settlement		$	$	$
LESS: Seller Held Trust, if not Sold		$	$	$
Other (e.g. rent back, walk through items, etc.)		$	$	$
Adjusted Net Proceeds		$	$	$
*POC = Paid Outside of Closing				

These estimates are not guaranteed and may not include escrows. Escrow balances are reimbursed by the existing lender. When a loan is assumed, Purchaser reimburses Seller for escrow balance at settlement, unless otherwise stated in the contract. Taxes, rents and association dues are prorated at settlement. Under Virginia law, Seller's proceeds may not be available for up to 3 business days following the completion of the settlement. Seller acknowledges receipt of this statement.

PREPARED BY AGENT _____   SELLER _____

DATE _____   SELLER _____

FHA Loan payoff: For loans originated prior to January 21, 2015, if the payoff is not received by the lender by the 1st day of the month, the lender has the right to collect interest to the end of the month in which the payoff is received. If a written notice is not given, an additional month's interest may accrue. Such notice is the responsibility of the seller.

© 2019 Northern Virginia Association of REALTORS®, Inc.

NVAR - K1307 - Rev. 01-19

What's Your Net Profit?

Chapter 14
Why use a Realtor?

I know with the "Make Me Move Buttons" and "For Sale By Owner" or "Military For Sale" or other specialty sites and Auction Opportunities you're wondering... "Why do I need a Local Realtor? I can sell my home myself" or "My friend, Mary, at the office is a Part-time Agent. Why not use her?"

Why not indeed. My question when using someone from work is two fold: 1. How far away is your office? Many people in my community travel 45 minute to two hours, one way to work every day. Do you really believe a part-time agent is going to check on your property weekly or daily? Do you believe they have a 'Buyer's List' for your neighborhood?

2. You work with this person. You know how many hours approximately they work with you. Add commuting time to those hours. How much time do they have to work their part-time real estate business? Do they have more energy than you do to put into a second job? I believe you're able to answer these questions for yourself. If that is the case... 'You get what you pay for.' You are using a 'part-time' agent, are they giving you a 'part-time' commission deal?

If you're Selling the Home Yourself: I have a few questions for you.

A. Does your Homeowners Insurance cover you if you are robbed by someone you let in? (A Professional Realtor pays for Errors and Omissions to cover unforeseen issues.)

As Licensed Professionals WE take Ethics every other year and our licensed is based on Honesty and Integrity. WE could loose our license if we're caught steeling from a Listing.

B. Are you going to take your own photos? Or hirer a Professional? Do you realize that photographing a structure and land is different than photographing a person? Perspective plays a HUGE Role in Photos!

Are you able to create a Video Tour on your own?

Do you know and understand how Fair Housing and Discriminatory wording plays into adds?

Do you know your liability in regards to these laws?

Do you realize how many do-it-yourselfers get into trouble via Social Media?

Do you know how to create a 'Virtual Home Staged House?'

C. You are responsible for storing personal documents on the sale of property. Do you have an electronic document storage? Are you able to electronically sign and allow the Buyer to sign electronically on a secure sight?

Do you have a professional Follow up system?

D. Are you going to vet every potential buyer before scheduling a showing? If so, do you have a plan in place as to how you will do that?

Are you willing to allow them to video or photograph your home for their absent partner?

Have you put away all valuables before they photograph?

Is your property now vacant? How are they accessing the property? If you use a combo lockbox, are you keeping track of who came and went? How do you know they left? How do you know someone isn't using the combo box in order to use your property to stay in or for a drop site?

Does your homeowners insurance cover illegal activity by an unknown party you granted access too?

When considering Selling without a Realtor please take a moment to consider the consequences and possible outcome. When you venture out on your own you take on all the Liability, and all the results of not having a professional mediator to look out for your best interest including financial and legal liabilities.

Chapter 15

What Many Sellers Overlook

For the List Makers I have an additional List to Consider:

Off the Cuff or basing the Sales price on What you Owe vs Due Diligence:
A Buyer isn't responsible for What you owe. That's your debt, not theirs.

I worked through Years of SHORT SALES AND BANK FORECLOSURES because Sellers wanted to hold out for what they owed in a falling market!

A Buyer is going to look at what the house down the street sold for regardless if it looks like yours or not. That Sales Price Will Impact Your Sales price in some way or another.

During the worst of the Short Sales I saw Appraisers use Short Sale Homes as comps to regular priced homes in neighborhoods that didn't have enough 'Regular Sales' for the Appraisal to have three comparables. In those case, the short sales effected the sales price and the amount the Lender was willing to lend.

A Professional Realtor will have done '**Due Diligence**' prior to your Listing Appointment. They will have created a 'Comparative Market Analysis' for your home that should at least provide a ball park range of value. This is your best source of value as they are professionals working in your properties area every day! They may provide a range and ask to view your home and property to give you a tighter range. A Professional wants to see for themselves what sets your house apart from the neighbors house. Value is not just based on square footage. It's also based on 'Quality.' Quality of materials used as well as the Quality of the workmanship involved.

> *'A few years ago I listed a doublewide with additions and an above ground pool. They had a lovely screened in porch and a one car garage with a little one bedroom in-law upstairs.*
> *Next door I listed a one level, stick built home with an 'in ground' pool and a wonderful three car garage!*
> *The Owners of the Doublewide couldn't understand why someone would pay $75,000 more for the stick built home next door before buying their wonderful cottage get-a-way.*
> *They did not 'SEE' that the quality of workmanship in a double wide with an above-ground pool did not compare to a stick built home.*
> *They didn't SEE why someone would prefer to pay $75,000 more to have granite counters and ceramic floors, and solidly built walls and energy efficient windows over their well maintained formica counters, vinyl and carpeted floors and thinly constructed walls, and windows.*
> *PREFERENCE is a selling feature!*
> *The doublewide sold, after the stick built home.'*

So, Let a Professional Realtor provide you a **CMA**. This should be your guide when pricing your home for sale on the market.

As a Realtor its distressing to see Seller's go with an Agent that agrees to their inflated price to hit the market. Did that Realtor explain to you that by 'Over Pricing' your Property you are in effect "Chasing the Market' rather than wading knee deep into the market?

Yes, YOU SET THE PRICE OF YOUR HOME. However, if you're truly ready to sell, you have sat with a Professional Realtor who showed you actually statistics for the area and a solid Marketing Plan they have had success with.

The Professional you chose should be knowledgeable, trustworthy, and able to answer any questions you may have in a timely fashion. They should be able to provide you confidence and whisk away any concerns you may have of the selling process.

Selling a Property is a Business Transaction:

You may find it difficult to be objective. You may not want to sell to a particular individual because you forgot this is a Business Transaction and for you it if TOO PERSONAL.

This is why so many Seller's are not happy with an agent after closing. When you ask them: Did you sell your home with that agent? They admit that they did.

Did you buy your next home through that agent? Again they admit they did. So, it's not that the agent did a bad job. It's the simple fact that they didn't have a good bed side manner when doing their job. For the Agent it's a JOB. For you, Mr. and Ms. Seller its an emotional undertaking. As an Agent I explain that the Selling Price is Subjective. The Sales Price is a Business Transaction between you and a Buyer. The agent has not lived in your home with you for the last ten years and therefore is not as Emotionally Engaged as you are. They are able to navigate a 'Reasonable Sales Price' with you based on the knowledge of your particular market and their experience.

This may also be where a Professional has to firmly and wisely clarify all your upgrades and general maintenance over the years may not equate in a dollar for dollar value to the sales price.

Example: Solar Panels may bring added value in the Mid-West or in Sunny California. They may be a nice feature with no additional value in New England.

Or You may have spent a small fortune on Windows, but they are not with a company the provides a ten year warranty, and therefore may be a nice fresh look, but not add any additional dollar value.

The prime example is the 'Above Ground Pool!' This is actually 'Personal Property' that doesn't necessarily convey. Therefore, it adds NO VALUE at all to a property. An In-ground pool adds 'A SALES APPEAL VALUE' not an actually DOLLAR for dollar value. And if the liner needs replaced it may actually take away value.

I CAN NOT STRESS ENOUGH HOW IMPORTANT IT IS TO PRICE A PROPERTY CORRECTLY FROM THE BEGINNING!
Unlike cars… Real Estate Sales or Discounts do not bring the BUYERS out in droves. A well priced home will bring the buyers.
You have to ask yourself…. Do you want to Chase the Market with a High Sales Price that makes you feel good? Or would you prefer to sell your home quickly by pricing it based on a CMA provided by a knowledgeable, local Real Estate Professional?

Many agents will win a sale by accepting your Over Inflated Price with the stipulation that you sign a Listing Addendum upfront agreeing to lower the price weekly or monthly to a point that is in line with the market. This is what I refer to when I say, 'Chasing the Market.' By the time they get you down to where you should have been in the beginning you may have missed the market all together.

LOCATION and TIMING are HUGE FACTORS IN REAL ESTATE!!!

UNDER PRICING IS AS BAD AS OVER PRICING!
Yes, I said it, "Under pricing is as bad as Over Pricing."
Why? Because you Lose Money on what is for most people the Biggest Investment of their lives!
I can not stress enough the importance of 'Due Diligence' in Real Estate. Not just when you look to purchase but also when you are looking to Sell. When you rent an apartment you are looking for the 'best price, in a particular location.' Best price is often based on the rental units condition. This applies to a hotel room, Air B&B or an apartment. You go in and look for a 'Move-In Ready,' clean place. When you're renting you are looking to see if your belonging will fit, where are the windows located, is it CLEAN?. You may be looking for a furnished apartment that is Clean.
The same is True for a Home Buyer. They are LOOKING at a particular Location. They are looking for a CLEAN HOME in their Price Range.   So, do not be in such a Rush to sell and move that you under-list your home or property!

Back in the Short Sale days I all too often saw a Lender allow us to List a Home as a Short Sale while also placing the house in the 'Foreclosure' Department. I have seen the Bank sell a home that was under short sale contract at a Foreclosure Auction for less than our contracted price because the Departments did not Communicate with one another!!

You read it right. A Lender may have a Short Sale contract on a house for $150,000.00, and it is in 'review' while they also gave it to their Trustee Department.

The house be foreclosed on and go to auction without even considering the Short Sale Contract in hand. I have seen such a case where the house sold at auction for $115,000! That's $35,000 loss.

Why would the lenders repeatedly take such losses? A. They assigned a Trustee at Pre-Foreclosure. This is a business to them, and it's about writing off loss or 'bad debt.' The Trustees cost is tacked onto the balanced owed by the present borrower. If there is a Loss at Auction it too is passed onto the present borrower in the form of a Note. If the home is sold for more than owed the balance goes to the present borrower.

Note: A Trustee is expensive. The result of Foreclosure is generally a loss to both the Present Owner (Borrower) and their Lender. A Short Sale on average equated to the Lender recovering more of the balance than from a Foreclosure. However, Foreclosure is still more popular than a Short Sale.

Why? Because a Short Sale is actually a longer process in many states. It is handled by the lender, and they need to seek the permission from their investors. There is a greater cost in employees for a Lender. Once a property is passed to Trustee, the employee cost is limited.

Under Pricing is as bad as Over pricing simply because it equates to less money in your pocket. That is a financial loss you may never recoup. All too often when selling a home privately the Seller turns to Online Home Value Estimates. These are based not on present market conditions in your neighborhood as they are in overall Algorithms for your town.

As such, you may not have properly valued your home because you either did not do your research or you do not know how to do the necessary research. PRICING ERRORS HAPPEN IN PRIVATE SALES ALL THE TIME! Knowing the true value of your home or property protects you and your greatest asset.

In addition to Pricing A Professional Realtor is also a **Professional Marketeer**! They have proven marketing plans to help you get your home or property SOLD for the Best Price! They have affiliations with **Professional Stagers, Professional Photographers, Professional Repair People, Inspectors, Contractors, Landscapers, Surveyor, Home Warrantee Companies, Insurance Agents, Title Professionals, Lenders and Attorneys**. In many cases some of these professionals may also co-market with your Realtor.

As a Private Individual you may or may not need all of these services in your transaction. If you do, you may find coordinating services can be daunting and time consuming. You may find there is no availability for you in the near future, however, should a Realtor call they may be scheduled right away! They have priority based on the volume of work they send that providers way.

For the Experienced Realtor they may make the process seem seamless. You may not realize how much service they actually provide or the number of hours they devote to your transaction. A professional Agent relies on their relationships in the community they serve. An agent looking for easy money rarely commits to a community. They make little effort to establish themselves or offer a solid marketing plan or working strategy to get your property sold in a timely fashion for top dollar. Take the time to interview a few agents in the location of your property or home.

These caring individuals quite often volunteer in their community. They are up-to-date on the latest housing trends. They have connections with local service providers to help you in every phase of your sale. Their Network is extensive and often features a Buyers List, Investors and Lenders that will help in the process. They often have relationships with other Brokers and Agents in the community and call upon them for their Buyers list as well.

These Local Realtors are knowledgable and may offer suggestions you for selling in your neighborhood that you may not have considered.

They are Organized. They pay attention to your needs, they love to communicate with you and they follow up on leads.

They are personable and sincere. Like many of my counterparts I have moved furniture for a photo, helped with Yard Sales, and arranged for yards to be mowed and hedges trimmed for a listing. I have even baby sat both children and pets for my clients over the years.

Realtors are Passionate! A true professional does not treat their job as a Hobby! They love what they do! Those that desire to be the Best at their Profession will seek designations. A designation is a sign they are sincere about their performance and profession. I have a number of designation after my name. For Example: The GRI is recognized throughout the country and in some other countries as well. This is the Graduate of Real Estate Institute. Less than 10% of Agents Nationwide commit to the intensive study required to obtain this designation. It means those that have are truly committed to learning how to serve their clients just as many attend college in order to earn a Bachelors Degree.

Successful Agents treat their career seriously! They didn't invest time and money to become a Licensed Professional as a Hobby. They have a strong work ethic and a desire to help others succeed. They are efficient and value time-management tools.

Career Realtors are Honest. They abide by the Golden Rule 'Do unto Others as they should do unto you.'

They are Self-Motivated and Independent. Even though they may work for a Real Estate Company they are generally paid a commission. Meaning if you do not sell, all their effort goes unpaid.

Creative - A Realtor must be creative to come up with effective ad campaigns. They must showcase each property they list. And be able to think on their feet and sometimes out of the box! They may need to adjust standard marketing plans to address special needs.

In today's Internet world they must be Tech Savvy. Ask them if they have a custom website. Landing Pages, or Squeeze Pages, Single Property Pages. Do they market on Social Media? Does someone help them manage their SEO? Do they have a 'Home Search' option?

As you can see a Realtor is a Jack of many trades. They often do far more than they are given credit for. They often work tirelessly to serve their clients and community. Are you proficient in Marketing, Negotiating, Consultation, Legalities, Property Taxes, Boundary lines, Title Issues. Are you able to gain the trust of Buyers, and service people you will need to complete your transaction? A Realtor works to earn their commission. Generally, that commission is split in some way with the house or company they work for.

Wrapping up:

Before Selling your house be sure you have a plan. Where are you going? Will you need another mortgage? If so, it is advisable to take the time to speak to a Mortgage professional to be certain you qualify for what you're planning. If you don't have a Mortgage Lender chat with a Realtor about considering selling and ask them to recommend a local Mortgage Representative.

If you plan to pay cash be sure to chat with your Bank. You will need a letter of credit from them as to how much you can afford. Or You could provide your most recent Bank Statement to a Realtor or Home Seller. Are you comfortable providing your personal bank statement to relative strangers?

Take the time to look at your current mortgage statement. You will need a mortgage pay-off when you should take a moment to call your lender and ask for the present pay-off. The Title Company will re-verify the pay-off just before closing on your property. But having accurate figures will allow a Licensed Realtor an opportunity to provide you with an accurate Seller's Net Sheet. They will ask if there is a Pre-Payment Penalty if paying off the mortgage early.

A Licensed Realtor usually has access to property tax records in general. They can provide accurate tax rates on the Net Sheet. However, they rely on you to provide the home owners insurance, home owners association or condo association fees.

They may also provide the estimate commissions. With a Net Sheet you should have a good idea of what your profit will be as well as what to expect in Closing Cost overall.

If the deal falls through do you get the Earnest Money Deposit? It depends on the reason behind the cancelation. If so, are you still going to sell? If so, will it be for the same amount, or would you like to adjust the price?

Can a potential Buyer be your buddy? Or would it be best to be discrete and remain at Arms Length until after the closing. Consider… Loose Lips Sink Ships. When in negotiations its best to keep careful council… and your cards close to your vest.

What happens if the Appraisal comes in low? Are you prepared to re-negotiate the transaction? Or will the Buyer be able to come up with additional cash to maintain the initial agreed purchase price?

Many People end up listing their property with a Realtor because they do not want to handle all the responsibility involved in selling a house! It's a big inconvenience to schedule a 'cleaning service' for a Deep Cleaning, perhaps some Remodeling, Painting, Landscaping, along with showings, phone calls at all hours, agents, etc.

Many Buyers prefer to see a house without the Seller around. Are you prepared to hear critical remarks about your home? Are you prepared to lose buyers because they do not want to deal directly with you if you're planning to sell on your own with a Realtor?

Once you have a contract the work is not over. You have inspections.. the Home Inspection, Well, Septic and Termite Inspections, If in an Association, some do their own inspection for each sale. The Home Inspection may make a request for additional inspections such as HVAC, or Foundation Inspection. Some Special Financing such as VHDA requires their own Inspection. If the buyer is planning to make changes after purchasing your property they may be applying for a construction loan.

If that is the case you may be required to have one or more inspections prior to closing for the buyer's lender.

You may have an excited Buyer that shows up more frequently than expected. Especially, if you are not using a Realtor, as a Realtor would reign them in. How comfortable are you with the buyer coming in when you're not there?

When you list with a Realtor you can specify that you only wish to deal with 'qualified potential buyers.' If you are Selling on your own, you will need to weed out unqualified buyers on your own. You will need to determine if you would like to offer Owner Financing. If so, how much of a down payment are you willing to accept?

Thank you for taking the time to read this book. I confess I LOVE to hear from readers. Whether you like this book or not, I would enjoy hearing from you. Of course, I hope you find it useful and helpful in preparing to list and sell your house. Did you find it useful? I am available in Virginia to provide you with a Comparative Market Analysis. If you're looking to list in my area, please give me a call to represent you as your Listing Agent.

What is Your Home Worth?

Give me a call to request a copy of your Free Home Value Report! Schedule an appointment for me to walk thru your home and provide an accurate Home Estimate for you to make an informed decision.

Please be aware… this Analysis is FREE without obligation. It is a service I provide whether you chose to work with me or not.
Upon request I will provide a rather in depth Market Evaluation based on your location of interest. Should you have any questions in regards to the report please give me a call. This in-depth report should help you develop an accurate value of your property.

As you may already know at Professional Appraisal will cost you on average between $300 - $575.00. My Market Analysis is pretty accurate of what the market will bared in regards to the value of your present property; and it's FREE just for the call.

I appreciate you voicing your interest in a FREE Professional Opinion on the value of your present home at this time.

Email me: tc4homes@icloud.com
Or Call: 540-455-1086

Please let me know if there is something I can do for you.

Best Regards:
T.C. Cooksley, Associate Broker
GRI, e-PRO, MRP, MCNE, SFR
With United Real Estate DC
P.O. Box 28
Boston, VA 22713

www.ingramcontent.com/pod-product-compliance
Lightning Source LLC
Chambersburg PA
CBHW020243290526
45784CB00003B/1089